College Funding Strategies
I Wish Someone Had Told Me:
The Ultimate Guide to Graduating Debt-Free

Dr. Christie Chamblis Murray
Nicole T. Cole, MBA

College Funding Strategies I Wish Someone Had Told Me
The Ultimate Guide to Graduating Debt-Free
All Rights Reserved.
Copyright © 2020 Dr. Christie Chamblis Murray, Nicole T. Cole, MBA
v2.0

The opinions expressed in this manuscript are solely the opinions of the author and do not represent the opinions or thoughts of the publisher. The author has represented and warranted full ownership and/or legal right to publish all the materials in this book.

This book may not be reproduced, transmitted, or stored in whole or in part by any means, including graphic, electronic, or mechanical without the express written consent of the publisher except in the case of brief quotations embodied in critical articles and reviews.

Outskirts Press, Inc.
http://www.outskirtspress.com

ISBN: 978-1-9772-2573-3

Library of Congress Control Number: 2020905199

Cover Photo and Design © 2020 Dr. Christie Chamblis Murray

Outskirts Press and the "OP" logo are trademarks belonging to Outskirts Press, Inc.

PRINTED IN THE UNITED STATES OF AMERICA

TABLE OF CONTENTS

DEDICATION & ACKNOWLEDGMENTS	I
ABOUT THE AUTHORS	IV
PREFACE	X
INTRODUCTION	1
COLLEGE FUNDING STAGES	3
COLLEGE FUNDING STRATEGIES	4
TEMPLATES	5
STRATEGY 1: TAKE RESPONSIBILITY	7
SCHOLARS	7
PARENTS AND GUARDIANS	11
STRATEGY 2: ASSESS YOUR FUNDING SITUATION	15
FUNDING SITUATION ASSESSMENT	16
FUNDING TIMING	20
CAPACITY TO PAY FOR COLLEGE	21
STRATEGY 3: KNOW THE COST OF ATTENDANCE	24
THE COST OF ATTENDANCE	24
VOCATIONAL AND TRADE SCHOOL	27
TWO-YEAR COLLEGE	29
FOUR-YEAR COLLEGE	30
GRADUATE SCHOOL	31
STRATEGY 4: CALCULATE YOUR ESTIMATED EFC	33
ESTIMATING YOUR EFC	35

THE SEVEN ELEMENTS OF AN EFC CALCULATION	36
DETERMINE YOUR FINANCIAL NEED	44
STRATEGY 5: CUSTOMIZE YOUR FUNDING APPROACH	**46**
TYPES OF FUNDING SOURCES	46
FUNDING SOURCES TO AVOID	50
CUSTOMIZE YOUR APPROACH	51
EXTENDED FAMILY OR OTHER CONSIDERATIONS	59
SPECIAL CIRCUMSTANCES FOR AID	59
STRATEGY 6: APPLY FOR FINANCIAL AID	**64**
COMPLETING THE FAFSA	65
FINANCIAL AID CHECKLIST	66
OTHER AID APPLICATIONS: THE CSS PROFILE	70
OTHER AID APPLICATIONS: COLLEGE SPECIFIC	71
STUDENT AID REPORT	71
UNDERSTANDING YOUR AWARD LETTER	73
STRATEGY 7: LOOK FOR SCHOLARSHIPS	**79**
TYPES OF SCHOLARSHIP ORGANIZATIONS	80
TYPES OF SCHOLARSHIPS	81
SEARCHING FOR SCHOLARSHIPS	86
COMMON SCHOLARSHIP SEARCH SITES	87
WINNING SCHOLARSHIP SEARCH STRATEGIES	88
STRATEGY 8: APPLY FOR SCHOLARSHIPS	**91**
SCHOLAR PROFILE	92

LETTERS OF RECOMMENDATION	98
ESSAYS	102
TEST SCORES	112
TRANSCRIPTS	112
TRACK YOUR PROGRESS	114
SUCCESSFUL SCHOLARSHIP APPLICATION STRATEGIES	116
STRATEGY 9: MAXIMIZE YOUR TIME	**119**
TIMELINE CHECKLIST (EARLY STAGE)	120
TIMELINE CHECKLIST (GROWTH STAGE, K-7TH GRADE)	120
TIMELINE CHECKLIST (LATE STAGE, 8TH GRADE)	122
TIMELINE CHECKLIST (LATE STAGE, 9TH GRADE)	124
TIMELINE CHECKLIST (LATE STAGE, 10TH GRADE)	127
TIMELINE CHECKLIST (LATE STAGE, 11TH GRADE)	130
TIMELINE CHECKLIST (LATE STAGE, 12TH GRADE)	135
TIMELINE CHECKLIST (SPENDING STAGE)	140
STRATEGY 10: EXECUTE YOUR FUNDING PLAN	**142**
COLLEGE FUNDING PLAN	143
GET ORGANIZED	144
CONSIDER YOUR COLLEGE FUNDING STAGE	147
CONCLUSION	**149**
TESTIMONIALS	**153**
APPENDIX A: WEBSITE RESOURCES	**159**
APPENDIX B: BOOK RESOURCES	**168**

DEDICATION & ACKNOWLEDGMENTS
Dr. Christie Chamblis Murray

To my sons, Kendall Devon Lewis and Kameron Tyrese Lewis, thank you for being my motivators. I pray that you will live a life of service and leave a legacy. May God protect and guide you through every aspect of your lives.

To my mother, Fannie Chamblis Bullock, thank you for your endless support. To my grandparents, Lamar and Flora Foshee, thank you both for your unconditional love. Thank you to my niece Alanna Porter, my nephew Seth Porter, and my cousin Sherman Grant for trusting me to assist with your college planning journeys. To my sisters Calandra Lee and Casandra Chamblis, my nephew Ronald Chamblis II, and my niece Jada Holloway, thank you for being my cheerleaders.

To my best friend, Felix A. Poteate II, thank you for your unyielding support. You energized me when I thought I had nothing else to give.

To "The Hampton University," thank you for providing me with a world-class education.

And most of all, I thank God for covering me, giving me gifts to make a difference in the lives of others, and shining a light to help me use my gifts for his purpose. I am humble and grateful for God's countless blessings, mercy and grace.

Ms. Nicole Cole, MBA

This book is dedicated to my college bound children Joshua, Journey, and Max. Be the producers and creators and own your success in life! It is also dedicated to my mother, Ms. Shirley Tarlton, THE teacher, my prayer warrior, and my unwavering supporter.

Thank you to my brothers, Charles W. Tarlton, Jr., and Dr. Edward L. Tarlton, for supporting me with resources, advice, and referrals to allow me to continue building The College Money Team.

I dedicate this book as well to the groups who built and updated my knowledge of financial aid and college funding since 1988, including the Office of Student Financial Aid at the University of Maryland, College Park; the College Planning Relief® team and Scott Moffitt; and all of my parent and student clients, who since 2009, have given me the opportunity to serve you, learn from you, and support you.

Last, I must thank God and my earthly prayer warriors and friends who even when I am not there because of all I have on my plate are always there for me.

Acknowledgements
Alpha Kappa Alpha Sorority, Incorporated® Members

We would like to acknowledge and extend a special thank you to the following amazing women of Alpha Kappa Alpha Sorority, Incorporated® who provided outstanding contributions to this book writing effort. We appreciate your time, efforts, and dedication. "We help each other!"

- ❖ Fannie Chamblis Bullock – Editing Services
- ❖ Shirley J. Cordell-Robinson – Editing Services
- ❖ Connie D. Glaze – Glaze Photography Services

ABOUT THE AUTHORS
Christie Chamblis Murray, DBA

"And I say unto you, ask, and it shall be given you; seek, and ye shall find; knock, and it shall be opened unto you." Luke 11:9

Dr. Christie Chamblis Murray, born in Montgomery, Alabama, is the youngest of three daughters of the Late Ronald L. Chamblis (LT, USN Ret.) and Fannie Chamblis Bullock. She grew up in Chesapeake, Virginia.

Dr. Murray is a 1998 Hampton University graduate, where she earned a Bachelor of Science degree in Electrical Engineering. While attending Hampton, she became a member Alpha Kappa Alpha Sorority, Incorporated® (Gamma Theta Chapter, Spring 1998). She earned a Master of Science degree in Computer Information Systems from the University of Phoenix, a Master's degree in Business Administration from Strayer University, and a Doctorate in Business Administration from the University of Phoenix.

Dr. Murray is a lifelong scholar who has a passion for learning. She has over 26 years of expertise in education, college consulting, engineering, business, strategic planning, leadership development, policy formation, public safety, strategic communications, public speaking, program management, and facilitation.

Dr. Murray is also the co-founder of Invest N Others LLC, an educational consulting firm, focused on educating and inspiring individuals and organizations to achieve their desired outcomes. She believes that knowledge and education are **POWER.** Her vision is to close the educational opportunity gap by providing college planning, funding expertise, and resources to those who need them the most. In 2018, Dr. Murray published her first book, <u>College Planning Strategies I Wish Someone Had Told Me</u> to help scholars learn how to get accepted into college and graduate debt-free. She shares her college planning and funding expertise with those in pursuit of academic excellence.

Dr. Murray co-wrote this second book, in her college series, to provide much needed college funding and scholarship strategies for scholars seeking to attend a vocational or trade school, two-year institution, four-year institution, graduate school and beyond. After speaking to thousands of parents, scholars, and others at national conferences, workshops, seminars, and webinars, Dr. Murray recognized the need for impactful information on how to reduce or eliminate college debt. With her two sons pursuing higher education, she recognizes the importance of finding ways to pay for college. This book serves as the ultimate guide for individuals and families who want to understand how to fund college, win scholarships, and graduate debt-free. May this book make a meaningful difference in the lives of those who ask, seek, and find!

Christie Chamblis Murray, DBA
Company: Invest N Others LLC
Email: author.christiemurray@investnothers.com
Website: www.investnothers.com

ABOUT THE AUTHORS
Nicole T. Cole, MBA

"For I know the plans I have for you, declares the Lord, plans for welfare and not for evil, to give you a future and a hope." Jeremiah 29:11

Nicole Tarlton Cole, M.B.A., born in Hampton, Virginia and educated in Highland Springs, Virginia, is a graduate of the University of Maryland and the Northwestern University Kellogg Graduate School of Management.

Ms. Cole has been a planner all her of life and believes in setting goals, writing strategic and tactical plans, and executing those plans to achieve success. She leveraged and built her planning experience after business school initially as a marketing and strategy management consultant for pharmaceutical companies, as an entrepreneur and as a business owner of a management consulting firm and an ice cream store franchisee. For the past 16 years, she has owned a college funding planning business, The College Money Team, and a separate independent financial planning business providing investment and wealth management services.

As a goal-based comprehensive financial advisor and wealth manager, Ms. Cole, recognized early on the need for families to achieve one of their most expensive, condensed term, financial goals – funding their children's higher education. Since most financial advisors focus on retirement, Nicole noticed many families were struggling to understand and receive guidance on how not to sacrifice their retirement nest egg or become debt ridden while still supporting their children during their college journey and beyond to gain financial independence.

After meeting with multiple families and hearing, "I wish I had met you sooner" and having to plan for her own children's college, Ms. Cole decided to start The College Money Team. This non-investment related college funding strategy and planning business combines her experience as a former Peer Counselor in the Office of Student Financial Aid at the University of Maryland, College Park, her Masters in Management concentration in Finance, her financial planning experience, and a unique opportunity to become a Certified College Funding Planning Specialist through College Funding Educators of America® (formerly College Planning Relief®).

Over the last decade, Ms. Cole has spoken to hundreds of families and organizations nationwide - at high schools, with youth and mentor organizations, with guidance counselors, and with college admissions planning firms. Ms. Cole has worked with many parents to create and partner with them to implement customized college funding plans for one or more of their students. She co-wrote this book to encourage more families to educate themselves on this process, begin to evaluate their own household resources and needs for funding college and execute a plan to achieve this specific financial goal.

Nicole T. Cole, MBA
Company: The College Money Team
Email: nicole@collegemoneylady.com
Website: www.thecollegemoneyteam.com

PREFACE

The purpose of this book is to help change the course of someone's life by sharing practical college funding strategies to cover the cost of college. Each individual must determine what college path to take and what resources and funding opportunities are available to assist with educational pursuits. The strategies presented in this book cover a broad spectrum of funding guidance and approaches. This book was written for anyone in need of funding to offset the cost of higher education.

Definition of a Scholar

A student is referred to as a "scholar" in this book. The goal is to encourage students to believe in themselves and to pursue academic excellence. The focus will be to elevate the college funding conversation. Anyone can self-identify as a student but this book defines a scholar as an individual who is deliberate and relentless in seeking education and knowledge and achieving his or her academic dreams with a standard of excellence.

Definition of College

Many higher education institutions require funding to offset the cost of college. The strategies in this book are applicable to scholars who need funding assistance to attend any of the following higher education schools:

- Vocational or trade school,
- Two-year college,
- Four-year college, or
- Graduate school.

Some individuals may not have financial shortfalls or challenges to fund their educational pursuits. However, other readers may want or need help with finding funding and executing the best approach to reduce or eliminate the out-of-pocket expenses needed to accomplish their academic goals.

INTRODUCTION

"I did then what I knew how to do. Now that I know better, I do better." Maya Angelou

Pursuing higher education, beyond high school, is an important personal decision. When making a decision to attend college and what college to attend, early planning can make a significant difference. Early planning could mean getting accepted into the college of your choice and finding enough funding to cover the cost to attend that college. Not all families can afford to pay for college out-of-pocket and many scholars and their parents end up taking out student and private loans.

According to the U.S. Federal Reserve, in 2018, borrowers owed almost $1.6 trillion in student loan debt. Student loans are becoming the norm in paying for college and the unfortunate truth is that student loan debt continues to rise and remains out of control. The staggering number of students graduating from college with student loan debt is unprecedented. In 2017, the New York Federal Reserve indicated that almost 3.2 million people, age 62 and over, were still paying off student loan debt. This is an indication that scholars must find ways to pay for college without being enslaved by debt. The key is to understand the college funding process and then develop and execute your funding plan.

Surprisingly, not all scholars understand the basics in the college funding process. While there are plenty of college funding resources available, many scholars struggle to make sense of it all. Either there is too much information available and it becomes overwhelming or it is not easy to find the right information at the right time. You may become overwhelmed or frustrated with the funding process and want to give up. But do not give up! It is never too late to start thinking about how to pay for college. If possible, start planning early. If you do not have the money saved or the resources to save money to pay for college, this book was written for you!

Recognizing that most scholars do not have all the information and knowledge needed or fully understand the process to successfully fund their higher education goals, Ms. Cole and Dr. Murray have provided their collective expertise help bridge the gap. Ms. Cole specializes in college funding planning and financial aid strategies using household and need-based resources. Dr. Murray specializes in college planning and pursuing scholarships to graduate debt-free. Scholars should use this information to develop a college funding plan to fit their specific situation.

College Funding Stages

Scholars and/or parents will likely begin the college funding process in one of the following four stages: (1) Early Stage, (2) Growth Stage, (3) Late Stage, and (4) Spending Stage. Each scholar, and/or parents, should identify his or her current stage.

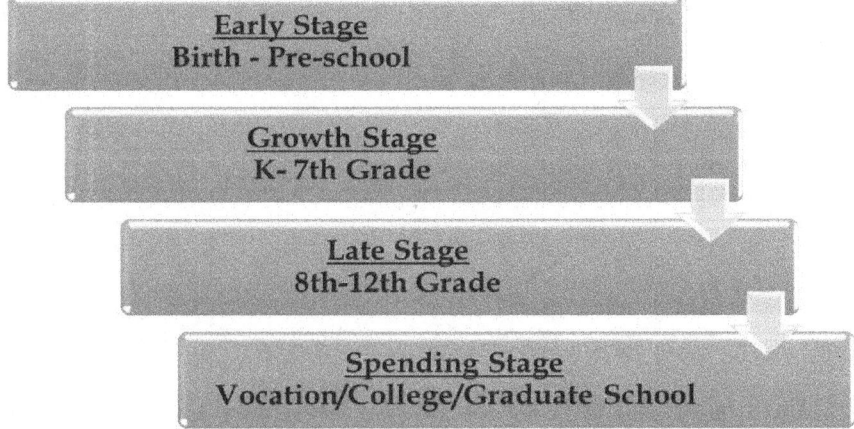

In the Early or Growth Stage, parents have more time to plan and save money for their scholar's education. Scholars in the Late or Spending Stage, are either preparing to attend college or are already in college. In the Late Stage, important college planning and funding decisions will be made because the scholar has a near-term need for college funding. If a scholar is in the Spending Stage, the scholar is in execution mode and has an immediate and ongoing need for funding. Based on the scholar's identified current college funding stage, scholars and/or parents should develop and execute a college funding plan using the college funding strategies below.

College Funding Strategies

Based on the scholar's current college funding stage and college aspirations, the strategies in each chapter can be tailored to fit your specific situation. These strategies provide practical step-by-step process to successfully develop and execute a college funding plan. The college funding strategies include:

College Funding Strategies

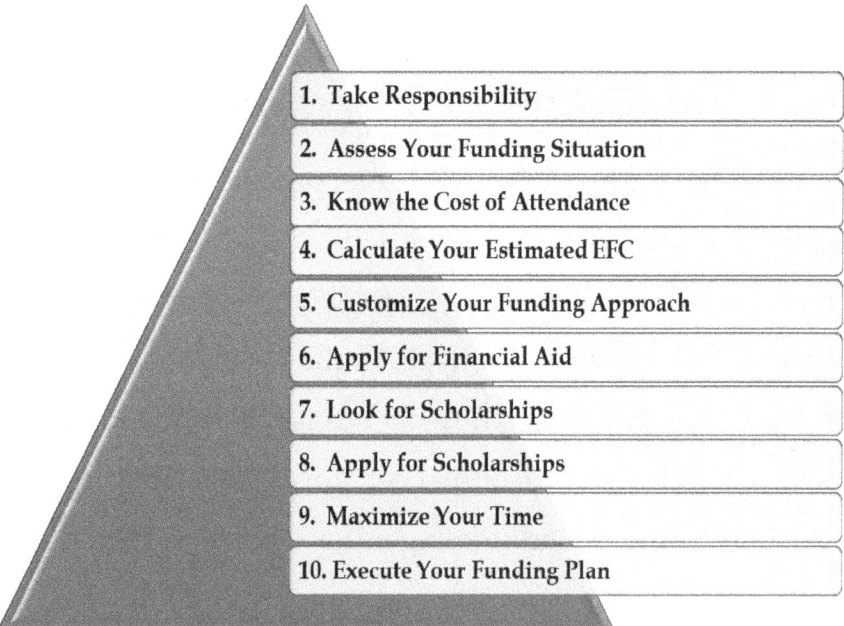

1. Take Responsibility
2. Assess Your Funding Situation
3. Know the Cost of Attendance
4. Calculate Your Estimated EFC
5. Customize Your Funding Approach
6. Apply for Financial Aid
7. Look for Scholarships
8. Apply for Scholarships
9. Maximize Your Time
10. Execute Your Funding Plan

Templates

This book also introduces and references templates, designated by template numbers. These templates provide practical examples or tools needed to develop and execute the strategies. These templates can help scholars write down and reflect on their funding actions.

- **Template 1.** Funding Situation Assessment
- **Template 2.** Calculate Your EFC
- **Template 3.** Customize Your Funding Approach
- **Template 4.** Scholar Financial Aid Checklist
- **Template 5.** Sample Award Letter
- **Template 6.** Scholar Profile
- **Template 7.** Sample Letter of Recommendation
- **Template 8:** Scholarship Essay Prompt
- **Template 9:** Funding/Scholarship Tracking Spreadsheet
- **Template 10.** Timeline Checklists by Funding Stages
- **Template 11.** College Funding Plan

Each template referenced in this book represents a partial view of the template. The full view of each template is online and can be downloaded and customized for your use from either of the authors' business websites at:

- **Dr. Christie Murray, Invest N Others LLC:**
  Website: www.investnothers.com/college-funding-book-templates

- **Ms. Nicole Cole, The College Money Team:**
  Website: www.thecollegemoneyteam.com/college-funding-book-templates

STRATEGY 1: TAKE RESPONSIBILITY

"I learned in an extremely hard way that the accountability falls with me." Stephen Baldwin

Scholars and/or parents and guardians should take responsibility for their role in the college funding process. Getting into college is one thing and finding money to pay for it is another. This is the first strategy because it a critical part of the process and it is important to get off to a solid start. Whether you are the scholar or a parent/guardian assisting in the process make sure you clearly understand your role and responsibilities.

Scholars

Scholars must take an active role in their college funding efforts. While scholars may or may not have the financial means to pay for college, they still have the responsibility to maintain good grades, narrow down their college choices and majors, be aware of how much college costs, and consider how much his or her family can afford. Each scholar should consider the following responsibilities:

Scholar Responsibilities

- Own the process.
- Keep your grades up and get involved.
- Invest in your education.
- Plan for college.
- Do your research.
- Look for college funding opportunities.
- Attend a college you can afford.
- Ask for help.
- Respect people's time.
- Work.

- **Own the process.** Do not rely on others to take the lead. You are ultimately responsible for your educational goals, outcomes, and funding. Do not put all the responsibility on others to pay for your education. Find ways to help yourself.
- **Keep your grades up and get involved.** Scholars should keep their grades up and manage their grade point average each semester. Also, scholars should get involved in school, leadership, and community activities. Academic

performance and extracurricular activities are typical requirements to qualify for scholarships.

- **Invest in your education.** While others may help you, invest your time and resources in your education. Those who are willing to help themselves first will more likely appreciate, respect and value the degree they earn.
- **Plan for college.** Start thinking seriously about life beyond high school or your current educational situation. Put together a college plan to better understand the steps needed to get accepted and fund college.
- **Do your research.** Understand the college funding process. Leverage the Internet. There is a wealth of information at your fingertips. The more you learn, the more capable you will be to put together a successful college funding plan.
- **Look for college funding opportunities**. Search for funding opportunities from various sources. Execute a plan that reduces or eliminates the amount of money you have to pay or borrow.
- **Attend a college that you can afford.** College tuition and expenses vary. You should select an affordable college that can help you accomplish your college and career

goals. Community colleges may be a great way to take courses and save substantially on cost. Unless you are paying for college without any help, it is not fair or appropriate to place the financial burden on others to pay for your expensive college education.

- **Ask for help.** Be proactive and ask for help. Talk to people and share your college goals. Your supporters may be parents, family, friends, neighbors, employers, college officials, and/or community leaders. You might be surprised who has connections, access to information, and access to funding. Be sure to thank them for their help.
- **Respect the time of others.** Time is the one commodity no one can get back. If you have partners/guardians and supporters to help you, be responsive and do not waste their time. If someone asks you for information by a certain deadline, ensure that he or she receives the information before the deadline. Never miss deadlines. Be sure to thank them for their time.
- **Work.** If you are planning to attend college or are already in college, be willing to work and to pay your college expenses.

Parents and Guardians

Parents and guardians play an important role if the scholar is dependent on them for financial support. While this book emphasizes that scholars own their college funding process, parents and guardians still have critical responsibilities. Parents and guardians should consider the following responsibilities:

Parent and/or Guardian Responsibilities

- Take an active role.
- Encourage the scholar.
- Know what's going on academically.
- Consider this a business opportunity.
- Do your research.
- Develop a plan.
- Determine the best college options.
- Budget for expenses.
- Set financial boundaries.
- Do not use your retirement funds.

- **Take an active role**. Do not leave it up to the scholar to get through the college funding process alone. Your active participation will make the difference in the scholar's college funding process.

- **Encourage the scholar**. As early as possible, begin saving for the scholar's academic future. If your scholar is in the Late Stage, keep them encouraged because it is not too late to find funding for college.
- **Know what's going on academically**. Pay attention to the scholar's academic performance including grades, GPA, test scores, activities, and timelines. The goal is to stay on top of these items so there are no surprises when the scholar is in the Late or Spending Stage. Poor academic performance may limit the scholar's ability to qualify for some merit-based scholarships.
- **Consider this a business opportunity**. Parents and guardians may invest thousands of dollars in the scholar's academic future and parents should expect a return on their financial investment. View this as a partnership and set expectations for the scholar to ensure they are equally vested in the college funding process. Partners have different responsibilities to each other and they hold each other accountable for shared results.

- **Do your research**. Find out as much as you can about college funding early. Use the Internet or contact a qualified financial or college funding professional to find out about savings plans, investment plans, financial aid, other sources of funding and tax advantages with which you might not be familiar. The more you learn, the more prepared you will be.
- **Develop a plan**. Help the scholar develop time management, financial management, and decision-making skills. Developing a plan to track actions, costs, and where the scholar is in the process will be helpful. The best thing to do is help the scholar figure things out by letting them think, talk it out, explore, research, and get as much exposure as possible.
- **Determine the best college funding options**. The scholar and parent/guardian should work together to determine the best college funding options. All funding options may require an investment in time, money and effort.
- **Budget for college expenses.** Include preparation costs in the budget for college. During the Late Stage, scholars will have numerous expenses before attending college. Examples of expenses might include: transcripts, college

application fees, travel costs for college visits, SAT/ACT registration and preparation fees, and more. Your budget should also include saving for the annual cost of attendance required to achieve the college goal.

- **Set financial boundaries**. It is imperative for parents and guardians to define boundaries with finances and set clear expectations with the scholar to clarify accountabilities and responsibilities. Stand firm and encourage the scholar to choose colleges that he or she can afford (with your financial assistance).

- **Do not use your retirement funds.** Parents, guardians, and adults should not pay for college with retirement funds and nor should they postpone paying into their retirement because they are helping pay for college. If you need more cash flow during college years, consider lowering your retirement allocation at that time and then increasing it after your scholar graduates. While college is important, your first obligation is to make sure your finances are in order.

STRATEGY 2: ASSESS YOUR FUNDING SITUATION

"Start where you are. Use what you have. Do what you can."
Arthur Ashe

Focus on where you are now. As you consider your college pursuits, start by assessing your current college funding situation. It is important to get a sense of the scholar's current academic performance and financial profile to gain a better sense of the actions that must be taken to graduate debt-free. Understanding where you are currently can help accelerate the scholar's college funding process.

Assessing college funding is similar to planning a trip. Determine where you are now, map out where you want to go, understand how long the trip will take, identify the best route. Also estimate travel costs including transportation expenses, gas, overnight stays and activities, etc.

To assess your current funding situation, you need to evaluate your timing, resources, and capabilities. If you are currently in the Late Stage, understand your college costs and create a budget for what you need to cover along the way for high school graduation expenses, transcript fees, college application fees, standardized test prep courses and registration fees, and the cost of attendance). The gap between your household income resources and the cost of attendance can be funded with outside resources. Matching the scholar's college plan, financial need, and the scholar's strengths will allow the scholar to focus his or her search on the Late and Spending Stages. Assessing your funding situation will help you establish a baseline for where you are now in the college funding process.

Funding Situation Assessment

To start, take five to ten minutes to complete the **Template 1: Funding Situation Assessment**. This is an assessment not a test, there are no wrong answers. It will provide useful insight into your college funding planning process in ways you might not have considered. If you are a scholar, complete the assessment based on what you know about your financial situation. If you are the parent or guardian of a scholar, complete the assessment based on your financial knowledge and needs.

Answer all of the questions honestly and skip questions you are unable to answer. If you do not know the answer off the top of your head, simply leave it blank. Do not be discouraged. This assessment is merely to help you identify gaps and opportunities to improve your college funding approach.

Template 1: Funding Situation Assessment

Funding Situation Assessment

Scholar Name: _____
Current School Level: ___ Middle ___ High school ___ Undergraduate ___ Graduate
No. Years Before Attending College: _____ College Funding Stage: _____
Type of College/Institution Planning to Attend:
- ❑ Vocational/Trade school
- ❑ Two-year College
- ❑ Four-year College
- ❑ Graduate School (Master/Doctorate)

Type of Scholar Funding Support (Financial Aid status):
- ❑ Independent (no parental help)
- ❑ Parental/Guardian support (parents helping you)

<u>Academics, Strengths, and Interests</u>
1. What is your current GPA? _____
2. What are your current test scores?
   - ❑ PSAT _____
   - ❑ SAT _____
   - ❑ ACT _____
   - ❑ LSAT _____
   - ❑ GMAT _____
   - ❑ GRE _____
   - ❑ MCAT _____
   - ❑ Other _____
3. What activities and clubs have you been involved in over the last three years? _____
4. What specific talents or interests do you have? _____

So, start by answering these questions:

- **Current School Level**: (Middle, High school, Undergraduate, or Graduate)
- **Number of Years Before Attending College**:
- **College Funding Stage:** (Early, Growth, Late, or Spending)

- **Type of College/Institution Planning to Attend**:
    - Vocational/trade school
    - Two-year college
    - Four-year college
    - Graduate school (Master's, Doctorate, or Beyond)
- **Type of Scholar Funding Support** (Financial Aid status):
    - Independent (no parental help)
    - Parental/Guardian support (parents helping you)
- **Academics, Strengths, and Interests:**
    1. What is your current GPA?
    2. What are your current test scores? (PSAT, SAT, ACT, LSAT, GMAT, GRE, MCAT, or Other)
    3. What activities and clubs have you been involved in over the last three years?
    4. What specific talents or interests do you have?
- **General College Plan:**
    1. Which type of college will you consider attending? (Check all that apply)
        - Public, in-state
        - Public, out-of-state
        - Private
        - Other: _____

2. What college(s) do you have in mind?
3. What college major(s) are you considering?
4. Do you plan to live on campus or off-campus?
5. Do you intend to play collegiate sports? If so, which sport(s)?
6. Do you intend to participate in scholarship eligible college activities? If so, which? (performing arts, creative arts, band, ROTC, etc.)

- **Household Finance:**

1. What is your (or parents) current household income?
2. Do you (or your parents) currently have a college savings plan?
3. If you had to start paying for college next month, how much money would you (or your parents) be able to pay out of pocket?
4. Rank your college funding concerns <u>in order of importance</u>:
    - Increasing cash flow/reducing debt
    - Selecting the right college
    - Paying off the mortgage or other debt
    - Keeping, spending, or selling existing assets
    - Student loan borrowing/working
    - Helping fill out financial aid forms

- Protecting your resources
- Searching and applying for scholarships
- Achieving financial security for retirement
5. Do you need additional college funding assistance?

Completing this funding situation assessment will provide you with insight into your starting point in your college funding process. This assessment is designed to expose gaps in your current funding situation and your college funding stage. It will help you and your parents/guardians (if applicable) refine your college funding approach to focus on what you need to spend your timing and your capacity to pay for college.

Funding Timing

Assess your funding timing. Reference the college funding stages to determine the scholar's current stage and timing. This will help you understand how much time the scholar has to plan and save money before the first college bill is due and the additional time the scholar needs to dedicate to this college funding process.

College Funding Stages and Timing

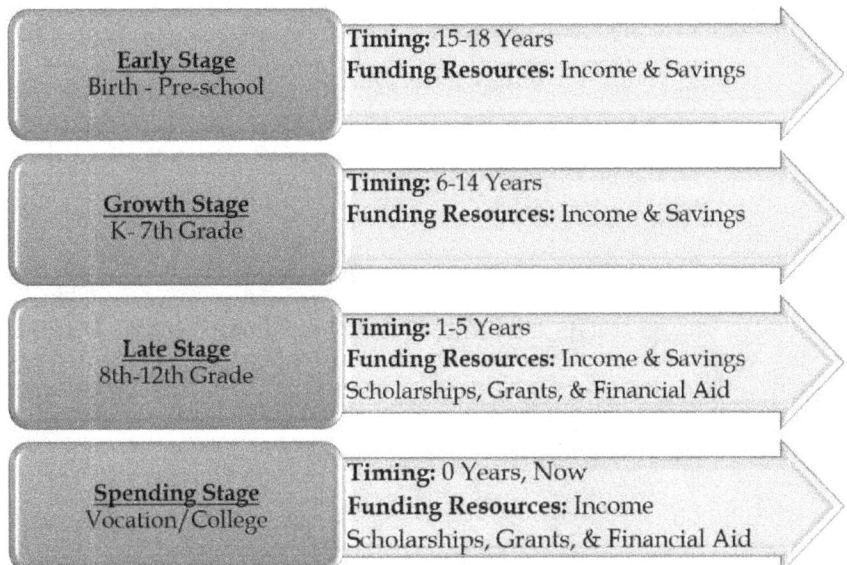

Early Stage — Birth - Pre-school	**Timing:** 15-18 Years **Funding Resources:** Income & Savings
Growth Stage — K- 7th Grade	**Timing:** 6-14 Years **Funding Resources:** Income & Savings
Late Stage — 8th-12th Grade	**Timing:** 1-5 Years **Funding Resources:** Income & Savings, Scholarships, Grants, & Financial Aid
Spending Stage — Vocation/College	**Timing:** 0 Years, Now **Funding Resources:** Income, Scholarships, Grants, & Financial Aid

The scholar and the parent need to commit time educating themselves, by developing and executing a funding plan based on their situation. The closer you are to the Spending Stage, the more time you need to dedicate each month to get the work done. You've heard the saying, "time is money." For this goal, this saying is even truer. Spending time executing the right funding planning activities should result in garnering more of other people's money to achieve this goal.

Capacity to Pay for College

Identify resources (either savings or income), to which you have access, to determine your capacity to pay out-of-pocket expenses. Some resources might include: scholar and/or parent income, scholar and/or parent savings (cash on hand, checking, savings, education savings accounts, other liquid assets), extended family assistance you can count on (gifts, trusts, education savings accounts held by grandparents, aunts and uncles, siblings). Considering what you revealed as far as timing, determine if you are capable of accumulating more of your own resources between now and the time college expenses have to be paid.

Estimate what you can afford to pay each month, whether it is $0, $500, or more a month. Thinking about how much you can contribute to college expenses helps. It will push you to think of and make the lifestyle changes required to be in a better financial situation in one, two, or more years. What you start sacrificing now may need to be your continued monthly sacrifice through to achieve your college funding goal.

In your funding situation assessment, only focus on what you know to be true about your current financial situation. After reading this book, you should be able to identify strategies to stretch your out-of-pocket resources and assess the potential resources available from sources outside your household to help fund college. The return on your time investment towards college funding planning may allow you to keep your resources for other years, other degrees, or other goals.

The assessment should spark your thoughts of other outside college funding sources like scholarships, grants, and financial aid. Your goal will be to look at your current funding situation and then take responsibility to close the gap between where you are and where you want to be.

STRATEGY 3: KNOW THE COST OF ATTENDANCE

"One of the greatest obstacles to escaping poverty is the staggering cost of higher education." Chris Van Hollen

The Cost of Attendance

Once a decision is made to pursue higher education, finding money to pay for college can be challenging. Without the financial means and resources to cover the cost of college, individuals may experience difficulties in achieving their academic dreams. Scholars must figure out how much college will cost and how to pay for it. The "cost of attendance" (COA) describes the total cost to attend a college for one academic year. The typical COA may include the following expenses:

- **Direct costs**: These costs typically have to be paid to the college:
    - Tuition and fees: The price colleges charge for students to take classes and receive course instruction.
    - Room and Board (if living in campus housing): The cost of living expenses for housing and meals to students.
- **Indirect costs**: These costs are not directly paid to the college but are incurred during the academic year. An

average allowance is projected by each college for these items.

- Books and Required Course Materials: The cost of textbooks, notebooks, paper, course materials, calculators, computer supplies, software resources, and more.
- Personal expenses: The cost of a scholar's additional living expenses including laundry, clothes, cell phone, entertainment, and medical.
- Transportation: The cost to commute to and from campus, trips home, or to work.

Some colleges are more expensive than others. The cost of attendance, for a particular school, may not be your price. The college costs you see posted on paper or a college's website are the college's "sticker price" and not necessarily your college price. While the sticker price is a number to start your cost assessment with, please do not stop there. Typically, there are other financial factors that could decrease the amount of the COA you will pay.

The cost to attend college increases each academic year typically at a rate higher than inflation. It is important to plan early to offset the cost of college and inflation. In 2019, the U.S. Department of Education, National Center for Education

Statistics estimated the average costs of undergraduate tuition, room and board, and other fees for the 2016-2017 academic year were:

- Public institutions: $19,488
- Private, nonprofit institutions: $44,702
- Private, for-profit institutions: $25,532

Your early research will help you understand how much different colleges may cost for you and how to determine what your specific cost will be for a particular college. Remember, your college funding plan has to be customized to your financial situation.

A scholar's college choices (the type of college, cost of attendance, and funding resources) are key determinants of how much money is spent on college expenses and how much of your wealth may be kept or lost. Consider that your college choice may have an opportunity cost. Opportunity cost is the loss of potential money from choosing one option over another. For example, Table 1 shows that if you decide to attend College A with an out-of-pocket cost of $15,000 versus College B with an out-of-pocket cost of $10,000, your opportunity cost for one year at College A would be $5,000 plus any earnings you might make keeping and investing that money.

Table 1

	Out-of-Pocket Cost
College A	$15,000
College B	$10,000
Opportunity Cost of College A	$5,000+Annual Investment Earnings

Consider the general cost based on the various college options you might choose from in a college funding plan for a vocational and trade school, two-year college, four-year college, and graduate school.

Vocational and Trade School

A vocational school, also referred to as a trade school, is an educational institution that exists to teach skills related to a specific job. According to the National Center for Educational Statistics (NCES), the average trade school degree costs $33,000. Still, the cost of one year of trade school will be dependent on the trade you are pursuing.

If a particular vocation is the scholar's desire, there are several benefits of attending trade school. Most trade schools are two-year programs. If the scholar is interested in a vocation in high school, he or she can often start trade school in high school while the cost is free to minimal. Scholars can and often do work while attending trade school and possibly, as a paid apprentice in the actual trade. The working income can be used to cover tuition and fees and room and board (i.e., rent to parents, if living at home). At the point where the student becomes an apprentice or intern in the trade, the company where the scholar works may cover the cost of materials.

Technical and trade school jobs have a median annual salary of $35,720 as of 2017 data from the NCES. The opportunity cost of pursuing a four-year college versus a trade school, if the career could be accomplished in either case, would be two years of salary from starting work two years earlier plus the cost of two more years of a bachelor's degree. The real opportunity cost can be upwards of $120,000 over two years. Table 2 displays the estimated costs for trade school tuition, fees, and timeframes. Additional COA for trade schools might be room and board, required tools, books and other materials (upwards of $2,000 - $5,000 additional), and licensing, exam and certification fees.

TABLE 2

Trade School Tuition, Fees, and Timeframes

Type of Trade	Cost Estimate	Time to Career
Electrician	$4,400 - $12,000	2 years
Apprenticeship	$250 - $1,420/year	4 years
Auto Mechanic	$10,000 - $25,000 (Associates)	2 years
HVAC	$1,200 - $15,000	6-12 months
Apprenticeship	$500 - $2,000/year	3-5 years
Pharmacy Technician	$500 - $5,000 (Certification) $10,000 - $25,000 (Associates)	6 months – 2 years 2 years
Dental Hygienist	$22,692 (Associates)	2 years

Sources: CostHelper.com, 2019; MidwestTech.edu, 2019; ImagineAmerica, 2019; CostOwl.com, 2019; trade-school.net, Aug. 2019.

Two-year College

The degree obtained from a two-year college, community or junior college, is an associate degree. According to the NCES, for associate degree students, the average cost of college tuition was $4,864 per year at public in-state institutions and $8,622 out-of-state. Private two-year colleges or out-of-state student costs were significantly more at $15,460. Most students at a two-year college commute, resulting in lower non-tuition related costs of attendance. The NCES found students who lived at home with family spent about $4,000 on average for living expenses. Those who lived off-campus alone or with roommates spent around $8,235 per year. Transportation costs averaged $1,780.

The range of total costs of attendance for a two-year public college was $9,289 for college students living at home to $13,585 for students living off-campus without family. For a private two-year college, the range was $20,306 for students living at home to $24,604 for students living off-campus.

Four-year College

A Bachelor's degree requires attendance and successful completion of a field of study at a four-year institution. It is called a four-year institution because the curriculum credit hour requirements scholars must fulfill to qualify for the bachelor's degree usually takes four years.

The actual average COA across four-year institutions varies significantly based on whether the college is public, in-state or out-of-state, or private nonprofit or for-profit. From the Average Cost of College in America: 2019 Report, the average total cost of college for 2017-2018 college year was $25,290 for public colleges in-state, $40,940 out-of-state, and

$50,900 for nonprofit private college. Factors important to add to your plan when considering the four-year program COA:

- Four-years may not be the norm anymore: The official four-year graduation rate for students attending public colleges and universities is 33.3%. According to a 2019 National Center for Education Statistics report, the six-year rate is 57.6%. At private colleges and universities, the four-year graduation rate is 52.8%, while 65.4% earn a degree in six years. This considers students who finally do graduate.
- College cost inflation: According to the College Board®, for 2014-2015, the average tuition increases for college programs was 3.7% for private colleges and 2.9% for public universities. However, a 2019 report from the U.S. Bureau of Labor Statistics revealed the average tuition price increase from 2000–2019 was reported at 5.14% per year as compared to the overall inflation rate of 2.08% during this same period.

Graduate School

Finally, how much does a Master's (or Doctoral) degree cost? Students can take anywhere from two to five years to complete a master's degree. A program's cost can vary wildly and heavily depends on the field of study and the type of college, whether public or private.

For graduate schools, the average cost is not indicative of what a scholar should plan to spend. If you want to incorporate the cost of a Master's degree into your college funding plan, we highly suggest you research this cost first, based on the field you are considering. Then, for the top 5 colleges in the field and which you might reasonably consider, calculate the average amount of time to Master's completion and the average COA for those colleges for one year. Using inflation, adjust that number based on how many years until you enter the Master's program.

Be sure to consider the increased opportunity cost of spending money and time to pursue a Master's in your field of study. For your college funding plan, compare that cost with the potential increase in income (your return on investment) and your competitiveness for future increases based on promotions or credible value (i.e., as a business owner).

STRATEGY 4: CALCULATE YOUR ESTIMATED EFC

"...thanks to a lot of hard work and plenty of financial aid, I had an opportunity to attend some of the finest universities in this country." Michelle Obama

Determining which colleges are affordable for you requires going beyond the reported college cost of attendance and understanding what **your** college price might be for specific colleges. To get an estimate of your price for college, you should calculate your Expected Family Contribution (EFC) and funding need. The Department of Education requires each scholar, seeking federal financial aid assistance, to complete the Free Application for Federal Student Aid (FAFSA). The FAFSA is used to calculate your EFC using federal aid formulas to determine federal aid eligibility. Institutions may use the FAFSA along with an institutional aid formula (from the CSS Profile application) to determine institutional need-based aid eligibility.

Ideally, it is best to pre-determine or calculate your EFC to understand your funding need before applying for financial aid using the **Template 2: Calculate Your EFC**. The goal is to have a rough idea of your EFC and need long before you apply to colleges so that you can plan your finances better. The more informed you are about your EFC and need, the better positioned you will be to find or save money long before you need it for college.

Template 2: Calculate Your EFC

Calculate Your EFC

Name: _____   Funding Stage: _____

Calculate your household estimated EFC based on your household resources using a calculator tool. When you apply for the FAFSA, your EFC will be shared with each college you designate. Colleges use the EFC as the base amount your household should be able to pay for one year of a scholar's college education. There are seven elements of aid calculations that are factored into the EFC calculation. Consider having relevant documents available to support your calculations.

Seven Elements of Aid Calculations

1. Parent income
    a. Taxable income as reported on your 1040 IRS tax filing
    b. Untaxable income and benefits
2. Number of people in the scholar's household
3. Number of scholars in college
4. Scholar income
    a. Taxable income, *do not include work-study income*
    b. Untaxable income
5. Parent assets
6. Age of oldest parent
7. Scholar assets

Use one of these tools to calculate an estimate of your EFC:

- Student Aid: https://studentaid.gov/understand-aid/estimate
- College Board: https://bigfuture.collegeboard.org/pay-for-college/paying-your-share/expected-family-contribution-calculator#efc_status

If you are uncertain about your situation and what to include in an on-line calculator, contact a qualified college funding planning specialist.

Your Estimated EFC: _____

Estimating Your EFC

The federal aid application states the EFC as an index number which helps the Department of Education and colleges understand your need for financial aid. The EFC is generally the main number relied on to calculate your need. It can be converted from an index number to a dollar amount to represent the amount of money a family should be able to pay for one year of a scholar's COA. For example, a calculated EFC of 12098 may be converted to a dollar amount of $12,098. The $12,098 may be viewed as the amount a family can contribute toward the scholar's COA for one year.

Using 2018 formulas, the EFC for the average American household with an adjusted gross income (AGI) of $50,000 will usually range from $3,000 to $4,000. There is no maximum cap on EFCs so some very wealthy families will have EFCs that exceed the cost of an expensive private university.

Calculate your household estimated EFC based on your household resources using a calculator tool. Consider having relevant documents available to support your calculations. Use one of these tools to get an estimate of your EFC:

- Student Aid: https://studentaid.gov/understand-aid/estimate
- College Board: https://bigfuture.collegeboard.org/pay-for-college/paying-your-share/expected-family-contribution-calculator#efc_status

If you are uncertain about your situation and what to include in an online calculator, contact a qualified college funding planning specialist.

The Seven Elements of an EFC Calculation

The EFC is not solely calculated based on household (parent and/or scholar) income or IRS 1040 tax filing. There are seven elements that are factored into the EFC calculation including:

1. Parent income (taxable and untaxable)
2. Number of people in the scholar's household
3. Number of scholars in college
4. Scholar income (taxable and untaxable)
5. Parent assets
6. Age of oldest parent
7. Scholar assets

Parent Income (Taxable and Untaxable)

Typically, the scholar will use the parent's income as reported in your base year IRS 1040 form. The base year for aid is the prior, prior year to when you will attend school. For example, if you are starting school in August 2022, your prior year is 2021, and prior prior year is 2020.

For the EFC calculation, parent income is generally counted more heavily than assets for most parents of dependent scholars. Parents' income can be assessed anywhere from 15% to 50%. Financial aid formulas assess a family's taxable and most income and benefits that are not taxed by the IRS. Among the items required by current aid forms are prior, prior year amounts for the following items:

All colleges count:

- Earned Income Credit (EIC)
- Additional Child Tax Credit
- Welfare benefits including TANF (not food stamps or subsidized housing)
- Social Security payments that were not taxed
- Payments in the prior, prior year to tax-deferred pension and savings plans (i.e. 401k, 403b, TSP, etc.) whether paid directly or withheld from earnings by your employer.

- Deductible IRA, SEP, SIMPLE, Keogh, etc. payments (not including contributions to Roth IRAs or Coverdell education savings accounts)
- Child support received for all children (not including foster care or adoption payments)
- Tax-exempt interest income
- Foreign Income Exclusion
- Untaxed portion of pensions (excluding rollovers)
- Untaxed portions of IRA distributions (excluding rollovers)
- Credit for tax on special fuels
- Housing, food, and other allowances paid to members of the military, clergy, and others
- Veterans' non-education benefits such as Disability, Death Pension, Dependency & Indemnity Compensation
- VA educational work-study allowances
- Workers compensation
- Untaxed disability income
- Untaxed portion of railroad retirement benefits
- Black Lung benefits
- Refugee Assistance
- Cash paid on your behalf

Some colleges (CSS Profile formulas) also count:

- Depreciation and losses on businesses and real estate
- IRS tuition and fees deduction
- Amounts withheld from wages for dependent care and medical spending accounts (i.e. FSA, HSA)

All colleges exclude:

- Child support paid because of divorce or separation
- American Opportunity and Lifetime Learning tax credits
- Taxable earnings from need-based employment programs (Federal Work-Study) and need-based employment portions of fellowships and assistantships
- Scholar grant and scholarship aid reported to the IRS as part of adjusted gross income including AmeriCorps benefits (including living allowances) and grant or scholarship portions of fellowships and assistantships

Some colleges (CSS/Profile formulas) also exclude certain expenses:

- Total of un-reimbursed medical/dental expenses based on a percentage of income (different than IRS calculation)
- Elementary and secondary private school tuition for dependent scholar's younger siblings up to a maximum per eligible child as determined by each school.

FAFSA and CSS Profile formulas include an allowance which protects a portion of the parental income from the EFC. The allowance depends on two factors: (1) number of people in the scholar's household and (2) number of scholars in college.

Number of People in the Scholar's Household

The aid formula applies an income allowance based on the number of people in the scholar's household dependent on the reported income. The aid application will automatically count the scholar. The parent(s) or guardian(s) and dependent siblings will need to be counted. Last, you will be asked if there are any other household members. Grandparents, adult siblings still living at home, or other family members living in the household who are at least partially dependent on the scholar or parent, should be counted as "other household members."

Number of Scholars in College

Aid formulas will adjust based on the number of scholars in college. If there is more than one scholar in college, the total EFC will decrease because parent resources may be spread to each college scholar. This prevents household resources from being double counted. Thus, if your household has other scholars who are enrolled in college or who will be enrolled at least part-time in college in the same school year as the scholar, be sure to include the scholar and the other scholar(s) in the "number of scholars in college." If the other scholar is in a Master's program, he or she can be included ONLY if he or she is filing for financial aid as a dependent scholar as well. Otherwise, they are independent and are no longer considered "in college" with this household. Unfortunately, you cannot count parents who may be in college.

Scholar Income (Taxable and Untaxable)

Many scholars will not have worked two years before starting college. So, this may not become a factor until their 2nd or 3rd year financial aid application. Also, the FAFSA formula includes a scholar income allowance. The 2019-2020 FAFSA formula protects dependent scholar income up to $6,660. This number increases slightly each aid year.

Similar to Parent Income, Scholar Income includes both taxed and untaxed income. So, even if the scholar did not earn enough income to file taxes, the income they earned should be reported as scholar income. Please note, Federal Work-Study, fellowships, and assistantships are need-based employment programs. Scholars can **exclude** the taxable and untaxable earnings received from those programs.

Parent Assets

For parents of dependent scholars, you must report asset values as of the day you complete the financial aid forms. The following count as parents' assets:

- Cash, savings, and checking accounts
- Any non-retirement investments including trust funds, money market funds, mutual funds, CDs, stocks, bonds, and other securities, stock options, commodities, precious and strategic metals
- Installment and land sale contracts (such as mortgages owed to you)
- Real estate other than the primary residence (including vacation property)
- A percentage of the value of business and investment farms. FAFSA exempts family-owned and family-controlled small businesses (or any part thereof) that have fewer than 101 full-time or equivalent employees
- Parent-owned Coverdell/Education savings accounts
- 529 college savings plans, and the refund value of 529 prepaid tuition plans for the scholar applicant and his or her brothers and sisters

Additional assets counted as parents' assets by CSS Profile schools only:
- Home equity
- Value of non-retirement annuities
- Equity in a family farm home and family farm business
- A percentage of the value of business and investment farms even when they are family owned and controlled and have fewer than 101 full-time or equivalent employees.
- Assets that are held in the names of the scholar's brothers and sisters who are under age 18 and not college scholars.

Age of Oldest Parent

The FAFSA will require the birthdate for each parent in the household. The EFC formula applies an asset allowance which reduces the amount of contribution from assets based on the age of the oldest parent in the household.

Scholar Assets

For "dependent" scholars, both the FAFSA and CSS Profile consider the same assets listed for parents, but which are specifically titled to the scholar. Typically, assets considered scholar assets would be:

- Savings in a Uniform Gifts to Minors Act (UGMA) or Uniform Transfers to Minors Act (UTMA) account – bank checking, savings, money market, etc. accounts with the scholar as the beneficial owner of the account.
- Trusts allocated to the scholar.

Scholars do not receive an asset protection allowance. Moreover, for the CSS Profile formulas, allow for a "sweat equity" required contribution from scholars of around $1,800. This contribution requirement is adjusted annually.

Determine Your Financial Need

Now that you understand the COA, which is different for every college, and estimated your EFC, you can determine your **financial need**. Your **need** is the amount of the COA you cannot afford to pay. For the financial aid "need-based" award, a college can cover up to 100% of your financial need. However, a college is not obligated to cover 100% of a scholar's financial need. The amount below a full need-based award or the difference between 0% and 100% is deemed "unmet" need. You will need to add to your EFC the amount of unmet need for each college. The key when comparing your total out-of-pocket or "net cost" for each college will be to compare the unmet need for each.

Formula 1:
Need = COA - EFC

Formula 2:
Unmet Need = COA – EFC - Awarded Aid

Formula 3:
Total Out-of-Pocket Cost (Net Cost) = EFC + Unmet Need

STRATEGY 5: CUSTOMIZE YOUR FUNDING APPROACH

"Stay committed to your decisions, but stay flexible in your approach." Tony Robbins

Now that you have calculated your estimated EFC and identified your financial need, the next step is to customize your funding approach. The purpose of customizing your funding approach is to identify how to minimize your out-of-pocket expense and/or maximize access to funding sources to cover the net cost. One of the first steps in customizing your funding approach is to understand the types of funding sources scholars can leverage.

Types of Funding Sources

Scholars can leverage numerous funding sources to meet their financial needs. There are two general categories of funding sources: household and outside sources. Household sources come from parents, guardians and scholar income and savings. Outside sources come from colleges, institutions, organizations and individuals not related to the scholar.

Household Sources:

- **Out-of-pocket (OOP)**: Some families have the income, savings, and or investments to pay some or all college expenses.
- **College savings plans**: Many states have specific college investment plans or pre-paid plans to help parents and scholars save specifically for college. These college savings plans may have state tax advantages and tax-free growth and can help to reduce the impact of inflation on COA. An example would be the Virginia 529 college savings plan.
- **Cash value in a permanent life insurance policy:** This type of insurance policy (whole, universal, or variable – not term) may provide the same tax-free access to cash value, low to no interest loans based off cash and face values and protection over loss of income if a parent passes before or during a scholar's college years.

Outside Sources:

- **Financial aid:** Money provided to help pay for college when a scholar's household can demonstrate a financial need for assistance or aid. Financial aid generally comes from various sources such as: (1) the federal government, (2) the state or local government where you live, (3) the college you seek to attend, and (4) private, nonprofit, or community organizations. There are generally two types of financial aid: (1) gift aid and (2) self-help.

- **Scholarships:** Gift aid from colleges, private, non-profit, or community organizations that scholars do not have repay.
- **Grants:** Gift aid from the federal or state government that eligible scholars do not have to repay (unless the scholar withdraws from college during the period the grant was awarded without finishing). Almost all federal gift aid will be awarded as a grant, not a scholarship. The most common federal grant is the Pell Grant. To qualify for a Pell Grant, the EFC will typically need to be very low, between 0 and 5000.
- **Student Loans:** Self-help money borrowed for college that must be repaid with interest. Borrow only what you need. For a scholar to receive a Federal Direct Stafford Loan (DSL) award, they must complete the FAFSA. A DSL program versus a private student loan from a bank will be issued in the scholar's name only. If the loan is not a federal loan, it will probably require a co-signer. The DSL interest rate is typically the lowest rate student loan and is

set by the U.S. Department of Education annually. It can be awarded in two forms:

- o Subsidized: The federal government waives the interest cost while the scholar is at least part-time enrolled in college. Interest begins to accrue six-month after graduation or non-attendance.
- o Unsubsidized: Interest begins to accrue once the federal loan is disbursed.

- **Work-study:** A self-help program where you can earn money by working on a college campus to help pay for college. A work-study award will reimburse the college using federal funds for the pay you receive from working a "work-study" eligible job. It is not an upfront award of funds. Thus, plan for work-study income to cover monthly personal scholar expenses just like any working income would.
- **Fellowships:** Graduate scholars may receive funding for a Master's or Doctorate to support their full-time study, with or without the obligation to teach or perform research. A fellowship may provide funding for tuition, a stipend for living expenses, and health insurance.
- **Education expense reimbursement:** A reimbursement of college education expenses can be provided by an

employer as a benefit of employment. There is a maximum amount an employer can reimburse which is adjusted by the IRS annually. An employer might reimburse qualified education expenses for the employee or the employee's dependents. The employee first incurs the expense then provides a receipt or invoice to the employer for reimbursement up to the IRS limit. Scholars whose parents work for a college may be eligible for tuition reimbursement at another institution, check http://www.tuitionexchange.org for a list of schools and amounts.

Funding Sources to Avoid

- **Retirement plans:** The goal for retirement savings accounts is to replace working income in retirement to cover your living and lifestyle expenses when you are no longer working. Because of the penalties assessed for using these funds before you turn 59 ½, the opportunity cost of withdrawing from retirement plans early, and the taxes incurred when distributed, accessing this resource for a scholar's COA is not recommended. This includes taking a loan from your retirement plan.
- **Consumer debt:** The cost of consumer debt (e.g., credit cards, personal loans, etc.) is typically higher than other

options. Debt service payments can be burdensome. In addition, not paying the debt back can damage your overall financial well-being for years.

It is never too early to start thinking about funds for college. If you believe you will to need funding to pay for college, you should customize your approach and plan early.

Customize Your Approach

Once you have your estimated EFC you can choose the best funding approach based on your household category. Your household category is determined by your EFC. Generally, there are three household categories:

- **Category 1**: EFC between 0 and the maximum Pell Grant eligibility. Pell Grant eligibility max for 2019-2020 is $5,140. This amount is adjusted annually.
- **Category 2**: EFC between the maximum Pell Grant eligibility and an amount less than the college's COA. Pell Grant eligibility max for 2019-2020 is $5,140. This amount is adjusted annually.
- **Category 3**: EFC higher than the college's COA.

Using your EFC, customize your funding approach to best suit for your financial situation. The **Template 3:**

Customize Your Funding Approach can be used to map out your approach.

Template 3: Customize Your Funding Approach

<u>Customize Your Funding Approach</u>

Name: _____ College Funding Stage: _____
Your Estimated EFC: _____ Your Category: _____

	CATEGORY 1	CATEGORY 2	CATEGORY 3
EFC RANGE	0 TO PELL GRANT ELIGIBLE* (I.E., ~5500)	~5501 TO BELOW SPECIFIC COLLEGE Cost of Attendance (COA)	HIGHER THAN COLLEGE Cost of Attendance (COA)
APPROACH	Maximum Need • Seek colleges that meet 80%-100% need • Strengthen Scholar Profile for admission • Pursue scholarships • Build savings for unmet need	Maximize Aid Eligibility • Seek colleges that meet 70%-100% need • Strengthen Scholar Profile for admission • Build savings with protected assets not reported on aid forms • Pursue scholarships	Max Savings & Cash Flow • Build tax efficient, growth investments, and protected savings • Pursue non need-based scholarships • Leverage low cost debt
BEST FUNDING RESOURCES	• Financial Aid • Scholarships • Current income (parent discretionary; student work-study; student earned) • Savings (non-retirement accounts; cash value in life insurance)	• Financial Aid • Scholarships • Current income (parent discretionary; student work-study; student earned) • Family support where available • Savings (cash value from life insurance; Parent-held 529)	• Scholarships • Direct Stafford/Student Loan from FAFSA completion (no other loans if at all possible) • Leverageable assets like cash value from life insurance • Family support where available • College Savings Accounts (529; Pre-paid state plan)

*Pell grant eligibility is adjusted by the Department of Education annually. Pell grants are federal aid; however, distributions are administered by the college annually.

Funding Approach for Category 1

If you are in Category 1, your EFC is low and you will qualify for the maximum amount of need-based financial aid. Do not assume you will have no financial responsibility. Consider the following questions to determine what your financial responsibility could be for each college:

1. *What amount of need does each college meet?* If less than 100%, you will have a higher out-of-pocket responsibility to cover unmet need.
2. *Which college choice will result in the least amount of unmet need?* The college with the least amount of unmet need is likely the most affordable.
3. *Are there colleges the scholar should consider that commit to meeting 100% of need? Is it likely based on the scholar's academic profile, he or she will gain admission?* If the scholar can gain admission, a 100% need met college would be your most affordable option. These colleges are highly competitive for admission.
4. *If there is an unmet need, what are the best additional college funding options the scholar can pursue to cover those costs?* The best options can be a combination of implementing an outside scholarship search and application plan, a payment

plan using current income, asking for help from extended family or supportive friends and mentors.

Funding Approach for Category 2

Category 2 families will qualify for some need-based aid, even if it is only the federal DSL. When you plan before Spending Stage you may be able to implement strategies to lower your estimated EFC before completing the financial aid applications. Category 2 families should follow an **Aid Maximization** plan approach.

Aid maximization means through the Late Stage you should use strategies to save in EFC efficient assets like retirement plans (i.e., 401k, IRA, Roth IRAs), cash value life insurance policies, annuities, and small businesses. Which assets make sense for your household depends on (1) Your need for use and access to the asset to cover out-of-pocket college expenses when they arise and, (2) The availability of the option to you (i.e. you may not own a small business).

If you are a small business owner, with less than 100 employees, you may have opportunities to maximize aid by managing your income differently. If this applies to you, consider seeking the help of a college funding professional.

Be aware, if you own real estate outside of your residence (i.e.., rental property, vacation home, inherited home) in your name (i.e. not owned by a registered business), it may count in your EFC twice: once as an asset (market value minus the mortgage debt) and again as income (taxable profit from rental income). There are occasions where additional real estate properties can push a family into Category 3, even if the equity in the property is not accessible.

Again, planning is key. If you find you have a special situation, engage a college funding planning professional for assistance. A good college funding planning professional, who understands financial aid, taxes related to college funding and financial aid, COA, and need coverage for different types of colleges, can be a tremendous help. He or she will make sure you follow the rules as you customize your college funding approach.

<u>Funding Approaches for Category 3</u>

If you find your family in Category 3, your household is assumed to have the financial means and/resources to pay for that college's total COA without the need for financial assistance. Many Category 3 families do not agree or have not prepared themselves to cover this cost. Some just cannot imagine using their assets and income to pay all of the COA. Families who typically fall in Category 3 have high household salaried income and or have high reportable assets. Whatever the case, there are approaches to consider. Assuming you are in Category 3, and cannot reduce your EFC to create need, follow a **Cash Flow Maximization** plan.

Cash flow maximization requires income and tax management to achieve the most efficient use of your money. Consider these approaches to maximize cash flow by the time your scholar's college bills come due:

- Leverage the use of scholarships and gift aid. Your scholar should seek non-need-based scholarship opportunities at colleges they are applying to and with outside scholarship organizations. Every dollar from awarded scholarships reduces out-of-pocket costs.
- Leverage federal DSL awarded. If your investment assets, including the 529 college savings plan, are earning more than the interest cost of a DSL, it is more efficient to maintain the funds in your invested assets as long as you can. Also, you can spend less out of your own assets each year, so they may last longer. Then, use your assets (and the growth) to assist in paying off the scholar's student loans if you choose.
- Leverage your business. If you are a business owner, consult your Certified Public Accountant (CPA) to

determine if you are able and eligible to employ strategies to reduce your income taxes to create cash flow. You might be able to employ and pay your scholar(s). Scholars pay a lower income tax rate up to a certain amount. They can save the income they make to cover the personal expense allocation in the COA. You may be able to otherwise defer income or increase your income deferral and maximize savings in tax-efficient retirement assets.

- As with Category 2 families, use the best accumulation asset(s) for your situation. Again, which assets make sense for your household depends on your need for use and access to the asset to pay for out-of-pocket college expenses when they arise. Consider accumulating college savings in tax-advantaged cash value life insurance and 529 college savings plans first. For suitable asset placement for your family, consult a college funding planning professional with a planning certification (i.e., a Series 65 financial advisory certification) and/or a life insurance license or who can refer you to a qualified financial professional.

Because Categories 2 and 3 are dependent on the college's COA, you may find you are Category 2 for some colleges and Category 3 for others. In the stages before the

Late Stage, do not worry. Be conservative and plan as if you are a Category 3 family. In Late Stage, when your scholar considers which colleges to apply, focus your strategy based on more current information. Still, you may find you are a double category family. But you will be better prepared to cover the cost of the college which places you in Category 3.

Regardless of your category, in your senior year and throughout the Spending Stage, follow these steps:

1. Complete the financial aid application process and all required financial aid applications as accurately as possible.
2. Complete them as early as possible after October 1st for a rolling college admission and before the Financial Aid Application "Priority Due Date" for colleges that assign a priority date.
3. Check your e-mails for confirmations or requests for supplemental requirements and respond as quickly as possible. Colleges may not consider your aid application complete until all requirements are met.

Even if your scholar is not planning on applying early to a college, still submit your financial aid application by the college's first "Priority Due Date."

Extended Family or Other Considerations

Because of the high cost of college many scholars rely on extended family for support. Often, there are extended family and friends who want to help. If grandparents, aunts, uncles or others want to offer financial support, there are better ways to receive these gifts so they do not raise your EFC. While they want to help, they may not realize that some gifts hurt your qualification for need. For example, trust accounts with parents or scholars as beneficiaries are reportable assets.

If at all possible, gift contributions should be received after you complete your financial aid applications. If they are received prior, they count as current assets or have to be reported in the CSS Profile as gifts. If family members want to help a scholar, the scholar should understand their gift approach or meet with a college funding planning professional to ensure the gift contributions do not hurt the scholar's chance for financial aid.

Special Circumstances for Aid

There are a few common circumstances where applying for aid may require additional consideration. They are divorced/separated parents, remarried parents, and independent scholars.

Divorced/Separated Parents

Without getting into the specifics of the scholar's parent situation, assuming the scholar's parents are divorced or legally separated (with a dated separation agreement) and living in different homes (with different addresses), the standing rule for which parent completes the FAFSA and CSS Profile with the scholar is the parent with whom the scholar lives greater than 50% of the time.

If there is joint custody without the ability to distinguish which parent has "greater than" 50% of the time, then the parents can choose whose income and assets to use. But only report one. The exception is when the other parent is a custodian of a 529 college saving plan for the scholar beneficiary, this asset's current value must still be reported as a parent asset OR an asset expected from a family member. Whether the non-custodial parent will need to submit his or her CSS Profile application for the scholar, depends on which colleges require a non-custodial parent application. If it's required, be sure to enter the non-custodial parent's email so they can receive a link to complete their CSS Profile application. They may also have to upload verification documents into the IDOC system (idoc.collegeboard.org) or forward them to a specific college.

If the non-custodial parent is estranged or not able to provide information, you will need to provide proof of this status to receive a waiver from the requirement. Check the collegeboard.org for information and to see the requirements for a non-custodial parent waiver.

Remarried Parent with Primary Custody

If the parent with primary custody has remarried, the household is now a two-parent household again. Both the biological parent and the step-parent's joint income (base year 1040 married filing joint) and reportable assets along with the scholar's income and assets must be used in the application. Be sure to include all family supported by both parents within the house as household members whether or not they are claimed on the base-year 1040. If the step-parent pays child support for their biological child or pays alimony, be sure to report the amount. If a step-parent has a child they support who is in college, then include that scholar in the number of college scholars in the household.

"Independent" Scholars

The majority of scholars applying for aid for their freshman through the final year of undergrad are dependent on one or two parents or guardians. Dependent scholars are assumed to have parental support while independent scholars are not. As a result, independent scholars typically qualify for more need-based aid.

However, federal qualifications for independent scholar status are not based on the scholar being mostly or solely responsible for their educational expenses. Scholars must meet one of many specific criteria to qualify for independent scholar status:

- Be 24 years of age or older by December 31 of the award year;
- Be an orphan (both parents are deceased), ward of the court, in foster care or was a ward of the court when 13 years or older;
- Be a veteran of the Armed Forces of the United States or serving on active duty for other than training purposes;
- Be a graduate or professional scholar;
- Be a married individual;
- Have legal dependents other than a spouse;
- Be an emancipated minor or in legal guardianship;
- Be a homeless youth; or
- Be a student for whom a financial aid administrator makes a documented determination of independence because of other unusual circumstances.

If you feel you have another special circumstance for aid consideration not addressed here, please seek out a college funding planning specialist for assistance in planning your aid approach before you need to complete your aid applications.

STRATEGY 6: APPLY FOR FINANCIAL AID

"Don't tell me where your priorities are. Show me where you spend your money and I'll tell you what they are." James W. Frick

Financial aid refers to "money to help pay for college or career school." According to the U.S. Department of Education, the federal government awards more than $120 billion per year in federal financial aid to over 13 million scholars. Each year, the scholar must complete a FAFSA to apply for federal student aid, federal grants, work-study, and low-interest student loans. Colleges use the FAFSA to determine a scholar's eligibility for all financial aid. After submitting a FAFSA, the scholar will receive their EFC based on what a scholar's household should be able to contribute to their COA for one year. The EFC is a critical number which is specific to each scholar and recalculated every academic year.

If you do not complete a FAFSA you will not be eligible for federal financial aid or, some state and institutional aid. Some scholars do not complete the FAFSA because they: (1) assume they do not qualify for federal aid, (2) believe the process is complicated, or (3) find the process difficult to understand. Do not assume that you are not eligible for financial aid. However, if you fail to complete the FAFSA, you will be ineligible to receive federal financial aid.

Additionally, in some states, you will still need to complete the FAFSA to be considered for state financial aid. Also, colleges and some private scholarship sponsors use the FAFSA data to determine eligibility for their scholarships.

Completing the FAFSA

Scholars who seek federal financial aid funding must complete a FAFSA at: www.fafsa.ed.gov. The FAFSA is released on October 1st of the year prior to when the scholar will matriculate. For example, if a scholar is applying to begin college in the fall of 2021, the scholar would use the FAFSA application released on October 1, 2020 for academic year 2021-2022. Provide accurate and complete information. Submitting your application online is secure, and your personal information will be safeguarded.

When completing the FAFSA, you will answer a series of questions. You can preview the FAFSA question worksheet at: https://studentaid.ed.gov/sa/sites/default/files/2019-20-fafsa-worksheet.pdf or visit the website for the current year academic year's worksheet. The questions on the worksheet are listed in the same order they appear with the online application. Be aware some questions in the online application may be skipped based on how you answered previous questions.

Financial Aid Checklist

To navigate through the Financial Aid process, please use the **Template 4: Scholar Financial Aid Checklist.** The steps in the checklist are explained below in more detail.

Template 4: Scholar Financial Aid Checklist

Step 1: Educate Yourself

Step 2: Estimate Your EFC

Step 3: Plan Your Approach

Step 4: Register for Your FSA ID

Step 5: Gather Your Current Financial Document

Step 6: Prepare Your List of Colleges

Step 7: Complete Your FAFSA Application

If the scholar is a senior in high school, this will be the first time you walk through this process. Then, you will need to follow the process every year the scholar plans to matriculate in the college the following year. If you are planning for your scholar, use the first three steps before your scholar's senior year in high school to prepare your funding options so you can potentially qualify for more aid when you do start this process.

Before Completing the Financial Aid Application

- Step 1: Educate yourself - Understand the key information you have to provide and questions you have to answer before completing the financial aid application.
- Step 2: Estimate your EFC - As detailed in Strategy 4, estimate your potential out-of-pocket obligation or EFC. At fafsa.ed.gov you can use the FAFSA4caster to generate your EFC or work with a college funding planning specialist to calculate a current estimate for you for free.
- Step 3: Plan your approach – Implement your funding approach as determined in Strategy 5.

Completing the Aid Application

- Step 4: Register for your Federal Student Aid (FSA) IDs – Since most scholar households will complete an online financial aid application, the scholar and one parent will need to register for their own distinct Federal Student Aid ID. This will allow the scholar to access their FAFSA application and electronically sign the form when completed. The parent will also need an FSA ID to upload their last year's 1040 tax transcript directly from the IRS and to electronically sign the scholar's application when completed.

- Step 5: Gather your current financial documents – You will need the information from the following financial statements readily available when you complete the FAFSA:
    - IRS Tax Forms for Scholar and Parent(s): Last year's IRS submitted tax form (1040, 1040A, 1040EZ).
    - W-2's for Scholar and Parent(s): Last year's w-2 and if applicable 1099's from work. Note some scholars do not have enough income to file taxes with the IRS (i.e., they report as "Exempt"). They still need to report their income from any w-2s and 1099s received.
    - Current Financial Statements for Scholar and Parent(s) such as checking and savings bank statements, money markets, certificates of deposit (CD), 529, investments and other counted assets listed in Strategy 4.
- Step 6: Prepare the list of colleges to receive the Financial Aid Application – Submitting your FAFSA results to colleges is free. Up to ten colleges can be listed at a time. If the scholar is applying to more than ten colleges, wait 48 hours after you submit the FAFSA, then log back in and replace the prior colleges with new colleges and submit

the FAFSA again. You will also need to provide the federal college codes or simply search in the FAFSA online application for the colleges where you apply. If the college or university has multiple programs or campuses, you should go to the college website, search FAFSA and make sure you get the right code/college description for your program.

- Step 7: Complete the FAFSA Application: Most scholar households complete the FAFSA online at fafsa.ed.gov. As of the 2020-2021 application process, the form is available on the myStudentAid App as well. If the scholar is not considered an independent scholar, one parent or guardian will need to complete the FAFSA with their scholar.

Selective Service

Please be aware that when completing the FAFSA, male scholars who are 18-25 years old must register with the Selective Service (www.sss.gov) to receive federal student aid. Some states require male scholars to register to receive state financial aid when applying to state colleges. If you are a male scholar and wish to register, check the appropriate "Register Me" box on your FAFSA application and your data will be transmitted to the Selective Service. Don't worry, if you are not 18 years old yet, you can select to be automatically registered when you turn 18. You can also register by visiting the Selective Service website at: www.sss.gov.

Other Aid Applications: The CSS Profile

Over 400 colleges, professional schools, and scholarship programs use the CSS Profile (https://cssprofile.collegeboard.org) to award non-federal aid. The CSS Profile is also an online application that collects information specific colleges use to offer institutional scholarship and grant awards to scholars. Participating colleges can evaluate a scholar's financial need and provide financial assistance. If the scholar has an SAT College Board account, the same credentials can be used to sign in to the CSS Profile account. The initial application fee is $25 for the first college (check the website for updated fee costs). Reports sent to additional colleges are $16 each.

If the college requires the CSS Profile, you must complete it whether you think you will qualify for aid or not. Many require submission of the CSS Profile for a scholar to receive non-need-based merit aid.

Typically, there is a document verification process the college requires to validate the information you entered into the CSS Profile. The verification process can either be through IDOC or direct with the college. Be sure to check the scholar's CSS Profile submission confirmation page for which process his or her selected colleges use for verification. Always save a copy of any submission confirmation page and read it to see if there are any key next steps required to fully complete your submission.

Other Aid Applications: College Specific

For each college where you apply for admission, be sure to check its website for whether it has additional aid application requirements. Usually, these would allow the scholar to be considered for college-specific scholarships or aid. Some colleges do not require the CSS Profile but do require a short college-specific supplemental aid application. Do not miss submitting this information by the deadline.

Student Aid Report

At the end of the online FAFSA application, the scholar will be provided a summary of their answers. Be sure to review and scroll down to the bottom and save a copy. Then, after you and/or a parent signs and submits the FAFSA the scholar will receive a confirmation screen. Print and save this information as well as your EFC will be reflected on the confirmation screen. Make a note of your EFC.

About 48 hours after receiving your FAFSA, the scholar will receive a confirmation Student Aid Report (SAR), by email or mail. The scholar and/or parents should use the information on the SAR to understand their need, capacity to pay, and funding approach. The scholar can also login to his or her FAFSA account to download or print the SAR. This confirmation report will specify if there are issues that must be resolved before the scholar will be eligible for financial aid. Scholars and their parents (if applicable) should review the SAR for correctness and update their FAFSA accordingly.

The SAR will contain five types of information including:

(1) Your EFC: Index number used by colleges to determine your financial need.

(2) Verification: If there is an asterisk next to your EFC, this may indicate the scholar's SAR requires further verification

(3) Data Release Number (DRN): a four-digit number assigned to your FAFSA application. This number can be referenced to make FAFSA changes. Protect your DRN and only share it with financial aid administrators or FAFSA customer service representatives.

(4) Loan summary: List of any outstanding federal student loans the scholar has.

(5) FAFSA Changes: Changes made to the scholar's FAFSA.

Understanding Your Award Letter

The colleges you applied to will receive your FAFSA information, specifically your EFC. The college will use the EFC as an index for the amount of money your family should be able to pay to cover their COA and to determine the amount and the types of aid for which you may qualify. The college will then send you an award letter outlining your resulting institutional and federal aid award. The award letter will describe your estimated cost of attendance and your total financial aid package that may include: scholarships, grants, loans, and/or work-study.

Scholars should expect to receive award letters by April 1st for the coming college year. Once you receive your award letter, it will be important to make sure you understand the information contained in the award letter and that you respond to the college before the deadline specified in your award letter. If you do not respond by the deadline, you may lose your financial aid. Read and review your award letter carefully to make sure you understand your financial aid options, terms, and conditions before you accept any or all of the aid offered. In some cases, you might be instructed to provide additional paperwork or documentation.   The **Template 5: Sample College Award Letter** below gives you an idea of the types of financial aid a scholar may receive.

Template 5: Sample College Award Letter

ABC UNIVERSITY

Financial Aid Offer

John Smith
123 Main Street, Boston, MA 02110

Cost of Attendance: $56,000
Cost of attendance includes tuition, fees, housing, meals, books, supplies, transportation, and other education costs.

Eligibility Factors

Our determination of your eligibility for financial assistance was based in part on the factors listed below:

Enrollment Status:	Full-Time Undergrad:	**Number in Family:**	3
Housing Status:	On Campus	**Number in College:**	1

A change in any of these factors will affect your eligibility. Please notify our office right away if any of these factors are incorrect or if they change at any time during the academic year.

Financial Aid Offer

You are eligible to receive the following assistance:

	Fall	Spring	Total	Check to Accept	Revised Amount
ABC University Grant	17,995	17,995	35,990	☐	_____
Federal SEOG	500	500	1,000	☐	_____
Federal Pell Grant	2,960	2,960	5,920	☐	_____
MASSGrant	800	800	1,600	☐	_____
Federal Work-Study Program	750	750	1,500	☐	_____
Federal Direct Subsidized Loan	1,750	1,750	3,500	☐	_____
Federal Direct Unsubsidized Loan	1,000	1,000	2,000	☐	_____
Total	$25,755	$25,755	$51,510		

Outside Scholarships/Resources:

Total outside scholarships and/or other education resources for the academic year, as reported by you:

$1,000 Computer Science League Scholarship
$500 Boston Karate Scholarship

This letter is for your records and does not need to be returned to us unless you would like to decline any of the aid offered to you. If you do not want to accept particular awards, or you would like to accept less than the amount offered, please indicate the revised amount on the line next to the appropriate award(s), initial your changes, make a photocopy for you records, and return the original to our office.

Comparing Award Letters

If multiple colleges accept you, review all award letters and compare your financial aid award options to make the best decision for you. If you have engaged a college funding planning specialist, they should be able to assist you in understanding, comparing, and prioritizing your options based on what your total "actual" out of pocket cost will be for each college.

There are award letter comparison tools available to help scholars to awards from different colleges. Here are some useful comparison tools:

- College Covered: https://www.collegecovered.com/award-letter-tool/
- Discover: https://www.discover.com/student-loans/calculators/award-letter-comparison-tool
- Fast Web College Gold: http://www.collegegold.com/applydecide/lettercomparison
- Fin Aid: https://www.finaid.org/calculators/awardletter.phtml

According to a Howard University Financial Aid Official, "when comparing financial aid offers from other colleges, it is important to focus on your unmet cost, not just the sticker price or the amount of financial aid you were offered." After reviewing your award letters, consider that the award may not cover all your expenses and that you may still have out-of-pocket costs. If there is growing concern that your family contributions are not enough to cover the additional cost, stay encouraged!

Options to Offset College Expenses

As specified in Strategy 5, there are many other options to consider to help offset the college expenses for you to finance the cost of your desired choice for higher education. Because there are numerous ways to offset the cost of college, you should apply for financial aid early because you want to leave yourself time to look for other funding. Conduct more research to find other funding sources such as private scholarships and employee tuition benefits.

Please note, financial aid can be awarded up to the total COA for a particular college or program. Whenever merit-based scholarship sources pay over the cost of attendance, the additional funds are considered income and are taxable by the IRS. If you receive financial aid and a merit-based scholarship that pays over the amount of need you show, most schools will require you to reduce your aid sources. If you are given the choice of which aid source to offset or reduce, always choose your self-help student loans and work-study, first.

Appealing Your Award

Most people are unaware that there are some circumstances where financial award letters can be appealed. Many colleges set aside about 20% of financial aid for scholars who may appeal awards. You might consider appealing your financial award under the following circumstances:

- If your income has changed since the "prior, prior" year tax filing because of a loss of employment or reduction in wages.
- If your household size has changed due to a birth, divorce or separation, death, caring for a disabled or elderly family member.
- If you have recently incurred an unusual or unexpected expense due to a medical issue (whether for the parent, scholar, or another family member), natural disaster or catastrophe (i.e. a house fire, hurricane, or flood).

If you feel you have cause to appeal an award, be sure to contact the college's financial aid office directly and as soon as possible after receiving your financial award letter, to follow the college's appeal process. Make sure you have documentation to support your appeal and meet assigned deadlines. Focus your appeals on the two or three colleges you are most likely to attend.

STRATEGY 7: LOOK FOR SCHOLARSHIPS

"My parents didn't pay for college because we all got scholarships." Kyle Korver

If you are interested in finding scholarships otherwise known as free money, this chapter is for you! As you determine the cost of attendance, financial aid needs, and out of pocket expenses, consider applying for scholarships to fund college. Scholarship awards are gift aid you do not have to repay. Since college can be expensive, scholars should apply for scholarships to offset the cost of college. Some scholarship organizations will pay for an entire college education and others will pay a portion of a scholar's college education. Scholarship awards range in amounts from $500 to tens of thousands of dollars. Some scholarships are non-renewable, one-time scholarships. Other scholarships may be renewed for more than one academic year provided the scholar meets certain eligibility requirements (i.e. minimum GPA).

Academic performance matters! Scholars with a 3.0 GPA or higher should NOT have to pay for college! However, the scholar will have to put forth the effort to find and apply for scholarships! Many colleges and outside organizations soliciting for scholars who have great academic performance but you have to find them and apply. Search and apply for as many scholarships as possible to increase your probability of getting selected.

Good news! Even if a scholar does not have a high GPA, he or she can apply for interest-based scholarships where they may not have to meet academic qualifications. Again, scholars should search and apply for as many scholarships as possible to increase their chances of getting selected.

Types of Scholarship Organizations

There are numerous organizations that award scholarships. Some include:
- Colleges, universities, institutions
- Foundations
- Non-profits
- For-profit companies and businesses
- Social and civic organizations
- Federal, state, and local government agencies
- Employers
- Individuals

Types of Scholarships

There are various types of scholarships available. Become familiar with the different types and search for scholarships for which you are eligible. Some common types of scholarships include:

- **Need-based:** Scholarship based solely on a scholar's and or family's assets and income or lack of income. The scholar must demonstrate financial need. Academic performance, test scores, and or athletic ability may not factor into the eligibility or determination.

- **Merit-based** (need-blind): Scholarship based on academic performance, transcripts, test scores, and/or other factors. A scholar and his or her family's assets and income are not the determining factor. The assets and income can be extensive and the scholar may still be awarded the scholarship.

- **Interest-based**: Scholarship that is not based on need or academic merit. A wide range of scholarships may be offered based on a scholar's attributes, talents, skills, and interests. Scholarships may be offered based on (but not limited to):

- High school attended
- Ethnicity
- Race
- Gender
- Left-handed
- Right-handed
- Leadership
- Veterans (spouses, dependents, etc.)
- Disability
- Vocational, career, trade schools
- Talents
- Performing arts
- Creative arts
- Technical
- Interest
- Hobbies
- Degree
- College major
- Community service
- Civic
- Employment
- Federal programs
- States
- Counties
- Individuals
- Professions

- **Military Service**: Scholarship based on an individual's or parent's military service. The U.S. Navy, Army, Air Force, Coast Guard, and Commissioned Corps offer numerous scholarships for military service members, veterans, spouses, dependents of veterans, and scholars. Also, high school scholars may be eligible to apply for Reserve Officer Training Corps (ROTC) competitive merit-based scholarships. In many cases, these ROTC programs will collaborate with specific colleges. These services all offer scholarship programs to help scholars reduce the financial burden of college.

  Service-related scholarships may provide full-tuition coverage, additional funding for room and board, books and fees, a stipend or all of these. These scholarships can be two, three, or four-year scholarships. Please be aware that military service scholarship recipients may be commissioned as officers and required to actively serve for a minimum number of years after college graduation. The application requirements, deadlines, and available funding awards may vary for each type of scholarship. Visit military service and individual college websites for specific details on veteran, dependent, and ROTC programs.

- Air Force ROTC:
    https://www.afrotc.com/scholarships
- Army ROTC:
    https://www.goarmy.com/rotc/scholarships.html
- Naval ROTC:
    http://www.nrotc.navy.mil/scholarships.html

- **Athletic**: Scholarship based on academic and athletic performance for scholars who desire to play collegiate sports. The National Collegiate Athletic Association (NCAA) must deem scholar-athletes eligible to play and receive athletic scholarship awards.

    NCAA members set recruiting and compliance rules and policies for college sports to benefit athletes. The NCAA has a guide to assist with understanding eligibility requirements at: www.ncaa.org. Over 1100 colleges and 110 Athletic Conferences are NCAA members. Nearly 500,000 athletes compete in 24 Division I, II, and III sports each year.

    Academic performance is just as, if not more important than athletic performance. Athletes cannot merely focus on sports performance to qualify to play collegiate sports or to receive an athletic scholarship. Scholar-athletes must meet academic requirements to be eligible to play collegiate sports. The NCAA has specific eligibility requirements for Division I and II schools. Division III schools usually set their own eligibility and academic standards.

Scholars who plan to play sports in college should get familiar with the NCAA eligibility requirements for Division I, II, and III colleges. As early as middle school, scholar-athletes should understand athletic eligibility and scholarship requirements to ensure they meet and exceed expectations. If you are in the Late Stage or Spending Stage, and you are not familiar with athletic requirements to play collegiate sports in college, you should take immediate action to ensure you understand your eligibility.

Scholar-athletes who plan to play Division I or Division II sports in college, must be registered and certified with the NCAA Eligibility Center (https://web3.ncaa.org/ecwr3/) to ensure they have met the academic and amateurism standards. It is recommended to register with the NCAA Eligibility Center no later than the beginning of their sophomore year in high school to ensure you are on track to graduate and meet the NCAA's initial-eligibility standards. If you are planning to attend a Division III school, you do not need to register with the NCAA Eligibility Center.

To be eligible to practice, compete, and receive an athletic scholarship in your first full-time enrollment year at Division I or Division II colleges, the college-bound scholar-athlete must meet all NCAA-approved academic and athletic requirements. Scholar-athletes will have to submit: (1) transcripts, (2) SAT/ACT or other test scores, (3) other NCAA requirements.

Searching for Scholarships

Scholarships are everywhere! The goal is to apply for various types of scholarships that you are eligible for because scholarship awards can add up! Eligibility requirements vary. Therefore, scholars need to review scholarship requirements to determine their eligibility before applying.

The scholars who research and apply for the most scholarships usually get the most scholarship money. Scholars must commit their time and effort to search for scholarships! Scholarships will not just fall into your lap.

Scholars and their parents ask frequently, "How can I get scholarships?" or "Where can I find money for college?" It is easy! Roll up your sleeves and LOOK. Others may help you, to some degree; however, you must be willing to help yourself and put in the most sweat equity. You know your background, strengths, unique skills, achievements, and other qualifiers. Make the commitment to search for scholarship opportunities consistently and throughout your college experience.

Common Scholarship Search Sites

Take advantage of the Internet to search for scholarships. Many organizations post their scholarship opportunities on their website. Legitimate search databases can streamline your search and save you time. You may have to create an account and build a profile but it will be worth it. You will be able to sort and filter information to get scholarships based on your eligibility.

Visit college and high school websites. Many schools will provide lists of scholarships or websites of organizations that offer scholarships. Also, here are some common scholarship search sites:

- Big Future: https://bigfuture.collegeboard.org/scholarship-search
- Cappex: www.cappex.com/
- College Board: www.bigfuture.collegeboard.org
- College Scholarships: www.collegescholarships.com
- EducationUSA: https://educationusa.state.gov/
- Fastweb: www.fastweb.com
- Naviance: https://www.naviance.com/
- Niche: www.niche.com/colleges/scholarships/?niche=niche-scholarships
- Scholarship.com: www.Scholarships.com
- Scholarship Owl: www.scholarshipowl.com/
- Unigo: https://www.unigo.com/

Winning Scholarship Search Strategies

There are some definite strategies that, if applied, may improve your scholarship search efforts. Consider the following strategies:

1. **Start searching early.** Begin your search for scholarships when you first enter high school. Complete the scholarship application as soon as you are eligible. The

earlier you start, the more time you will have to research and fill out scholarship applications.

2. **Track your scholarship opportunities.** As you find scholarships, keep an electronic and/or paper file with the information on each scholarship. Also, pay close attention to the deadlines. Use the *Funding/Scholarship Tracking Spreadsheet* (**Template 9**) to track scholarships.

3. **Set aside time each day.** For scholars in the Late and Spending Stage, plan to spend at least 15-30 minutes a day searching and applying for scholarships. The best way to commit yourself is to develop a plan as to when, what, and how you will apply.

4. **Share your intent with others.** Talk to your high school counselors/officials, family, friends, and employers and ask if they have scholarship sources and contacts.

5. **Look for local community scholarships**. These are great ways to secure funding because many scholars may not know about these opportunities and there may only be a few applicants for each scholarship.

6. **Look beyond your GPA.** Do not assume that you must have a 4.0 GPA to qualify for scholarships. There are many types of scholarships that do not take grades into account.

7. **Network.** Personal connections can make a huge difference in winning a scholarship. Most people do not pay attention to the relationships they have with school counselors, family members, friends, employers, community leaders, and businesses. Ask those you encounter every day about any scholarship opportunities with which they may be familiar. Share with them that you seek to attend college and you are looking for scholarships to help pay for college. Keep in mind that local scholarships may not be well advertised. These are great scholarship opportunities because few scholars apply. This may increase your likelihood of getting selected.

8. **Take advantage of scholarship contest opportunities**. Scholars can earn money for interest-based funding opportunities. Some organizations offer monetary awards for arts, poetry, video/film, technology, inventions, business plans, social media, pageants, safety campaigns, and more.

STRATEGY 8: APPLY FOR SCHOLARSHIPS

"It's only after you've stepped outside your comfort zone that you begin to change, grow, and transform." Roy T. Bennett

The best way to receive a scholarship award is to apply. Surprisingly, scholars can apply for scholarships as early as their Growth Stage. Scholarship application requirements and instructions may vary, so pay attention to the details. The earlier you begin to actively manage and develop the key parts of a scholarship application the more competitive you will be when applying for scholarships. Some scholarships may contain some or all of the following parts:

Scholarship Application Parts

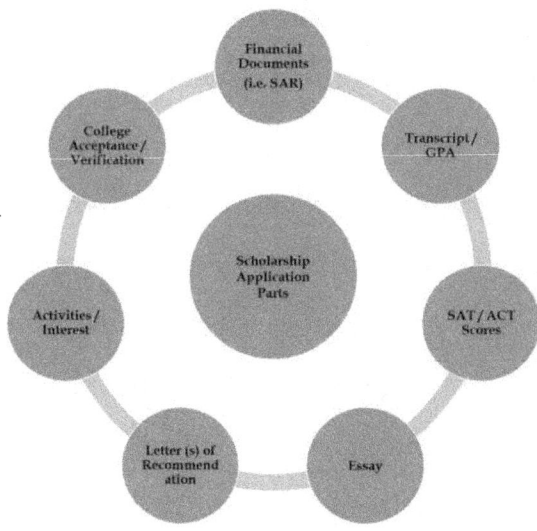

As you apply for scholarships, get organized and consider these helpful tips:

- Complete a draft of your application on paper before developing a final application.
- Follow all instructions on the application.
- If possible, type all applications (unless otherwise specified on the application).
- Attach all required additional information to the application. Consider attaching a copy of your *Scholar Profile* to set yourself apart from the competition.
- Review your application for completeness, and editing.
- Have someone review your application.
- Save a copy of all applications before submitting them.
- Submit your application before the deadline.

Scholar Profile

Develop a **Template 6: Scholar Profile** to market yourself and to help others learn more about you in a one-page summary. This profile is similar to a resume, but it is different in that it will help you to highlight your best qualities and leverage your strengths when submitting scholarship applications. Scholarship organizations may receive applications from scholars across the country and around the world. First impressions are lasting impressions. By developing a scholar profile, you have a unique opportunity to differentiate yourself from the competition on paper. The *Scholar Profile* tells the story of "you" and highlights your talents and abilities. Developing a *Scholar Profile* can help you market yourself in numerous ways:

- Letters of Recommendation – As you request letters of recommendation, you can provide your Scholar Profile to the individual (guidance counselor, teacher, employer, coach, mentor, etc.) writing the letter of recommendation. Regardless of how familiar you are to the person writing your recommendation, the Scholar Profile will help them to know you differently, and it will make it easier for them to write a letter of recommendation for you.
- Scholarship Applications – The *Scholar Profile* is also useful to complete scholarship applications. Besides, it can be attached to scholarship applications to help you stand out from other applicants.

The *Scholar Profile* is a simple one-page document that tells others who you are, what your goals are, and what you have accomplished. Use the *Scholar Profile* template to tailor it to your interests and experiences.

Template 6: Scholar Profile

SCHOLAR PROFILE

John Doe
12345 College Bound Drive
City, State Zip Code
Home: (123) 456-789; Mobile: (123) 911-4111
Email: john.doe@yahoo.com

Objective: To attend XX university and obtain a degree in XX.

Education: **High School**: XX High School, City, State (Graduation: 06/13/20XX)
Current GPA: 3.6; Rank: 29/283
ACT Scores: Composite: 24; English (24); Math (30); Reading (21); Science (20)
College Plan: Hampton University (Accepted on 1/20/20XX)
Enrollment Date: Fall 2018
Intended Degree/Major: Bachelor of XX in XX

Honors and Awards:
- Honor Roll, (20XX - Present)
- National Honor Society Induction, 20XX
- Top Alternate Current/Direct Current Student, (20XX-20XX)

Employment Experience:
- Cashier, McDonalds, City, VA (20XX-20XX)
- Walmart Cashier, City, VA (20XX)

Student Organizations/Extracurricular Activities:
- Student Government Association Class Representative, (20XX-Present)
- National Honor Society, (20XX-Present)
- Future Business Leaders of America Member, (20XX-20XX)

Community Service Activities:
- Alpha Kappa Alpha Sorority, Incorporated, Adopt a Highway Project, (20XX)
- Volunteered at Galleria Mall on Summer Family Nights, (20XX)
- Volunteered at the XX Community Center, (20XX)

Relevant Courses:
- Algebra II
- Graphics Design I
- Oceanography

Interests/Hobbies:

- Cooking
- Reading

At a minimum, a *Scholar Profile* should include the following:

- Contact information - Name, address, email, and phone number. Use your name and not a nickname. Also, use an appropriate email address that does not distract from your official business purpose (to get into college or get a scholarship).

- Objective (for college) – Provide a concise statement that tells the reader more about your college aspirations. Consider sharing what type of college you are interested in, what program or major you wish to study, or your career aspiration.

- Educational history (summary) – Specify the high school you attend, the address, your GPA, and your anticipated graduation date. Also, specify your SAT/ACT results.

- Honors and awards – List your academic, extra-curricular, and athletic honors and awards. Specify the year you received them. List your most current honor/award first and list the remaining honors/awards in descending order, by date.

- Employment history – Specify your job or employment history. College admission professionals like to see if a scholar is well-rounded and has a work ethic. List your most current job first and list the remaining experiences in descending order, by date.

- Student organizations/extra-curricular activities – List student organizations and other extra-curricular activities you have participated in since your freshman year. Specify if you were a member or if you held a leadership role. List your most current activity first and list the remaining activities in descending order, by date.

- Community service activities – Specify any community service or volunteer work on which you participated since your freshman year. List your most current activity first and list the remaining activities in descending order, by date. College admission professionals strongly consider community service.

- Relevant coursework – List relevant courses and/or challenging courses you have taken, such as AP courses that may interest the scholarship committee. Do not list every course on your high school transcript. Specify courses you took that might highlight why you might be a good fit for a particular college program. For example,

if you are interested in an engineering program, you might highlight math, science, and technical courses taken.
- Talents/Interests/hobbies – Include any talents, interests, and hobbies you have that might be useful to include.
- A professional photo (optional) – Include a professional photo of yourself. If you do not have a professional photo, take a photo wearing a suit, white shirt and tie or a simple solid color dress. Your photo should help you set a good first impression. Providing a photo is optional. In some cases, photos may be used to discriminate against applicants or candidates based on how a scholar looks or other perceived biases. If you have concerns that adding your photo may not be helpful or that it may be used to discriminate against you, do not include one.

When you first develop your *Scholar Profile*, you may notice gaps in some areas. The earlier you develop a *Scholar Profile* in high school years, the more time you will have to address any gaps you may have. You will have time to improve your GPA, participate in clubs and activities, take on leadership roles, volunteer in your community, adjust to take more rigorous courses, or retake the SAT or ACT to improve your score. Understand that as you develop a *Scholar Profile*, you will revise it often. Each time you review your *Scholar Profile,* you will find that you need to update information because you will have new accomplishments, experiences, courses, and activities to include.

A *Scholar Profile* will help differentiate you from potential competition. It will also help you organize your accomplishments and tell the story of you. When you apply to colleges and for scholarships, the last thing you want is to spend unnecessary time attempting to recall details included on your *Scholar Profile*. Developing and updating your *Scholar Profile* will save tremendous time and energy.

Letters of Recommendation

Scholarship organizations may require you to submit letters of recommendation with scholarship applications. Also, as the scholar participates in activities and classes, identify adults who may be able to write you a letter of recommendation when needed. Obtain their contact information (organization name, title, phone number, and email address) early on so that you can revisit with them later.

Strong letters of recommendation from trusted references can help differentiate you from other scholarship applicants. Read each scholarship application's instructions carefully to ensure you know how many letters of recommendation are needed, what types of letters of recommendation, and how each entity would like the letters of recommendation submitted. Some scholarship requirements indicate they would like letters of recommendation on a particular subject or from a specific type of teacher, guidance/school counselor or other professional. Use the **Template 7: Sample Letter of Recommendation** to get more ideas on what should be included in a letter of recommendation. Consider developing a merit-based letter of recommendation and a needs-based letter of recommendation.

Some scholarship organizations will send a link to potential recommenders for them to electronically attach or send their letters of recommendation to the entity directly. Additionally, the scholarship entity may provide an option for the scholar to waive their ability to view or access to the final recommendation letter.

Template 7: Sample Letter of Recommendation

_____ [Month Day, Year]

To _____ [Scholarship Entity Selection Committee]:

I, _____[First Name and Last Name], with _____[Organization], I am writing this letter to express my support for _____[Scholar First and Last Name] and _____[his or her] application for the _____ [Name of Scholarship]. _____ [He or She] plans to attend_____ [College or University] to major in _____ [College major]. _____ [He or She] demonstrated exceptional _____ [academic achievement]. _____ [Scholar Name] currently has a ____ [grade point average] at _____ [XX High School]. _____ [He or she] pursues academic excellence and welcomes challenges.

I have known _____ [Scholar First Name] for ___ [no. of years] years (or since 20XX). _____ [He or She] _____ [studied, worked or volunteered] with _____ [Organization Name] from _____ to _____ [Month 20XX to Month 20XX]. _____ [Scholar First Name] is extremely hard working and displays sound judgement required for a leader. _____ [He or she] is an individual with strong character and carries ____ [himself or herself] in a polite, respectable, and professional manner.

_____ [He or she] impressed me with ___ [his or her] ability to _____, _____, and _____ [solve problems, communicate effectively, and think critically]. _____'s [Scholar First Name] creativity and innovative mindset exceeded my expectations. _____ [He or she] was extremely _____ [proactive], _____ [professional] and _____[results-driven].

Without reservation, I strongly recommend _____ [Scholar First Name] as a candidate for your scholarship. Please afford _____ [him or her] the opportunity to continue to excel academically in college. If you have questions, please do not hesitate to contact me at: _____ [Phone Number] or _____ [email address].

Best Regards,

[Your Signature]
Name
Title

Useful Scholarship Letter of Recommendation Strategies

- Request letters of recommendation from individuals who you believe would provide you with a good reference and provide any specific instructions the college may require.
- Start identifying high school teachers who may be willing to write a letter of recommendation.
- Keep a list of teachers, coaches, group leaders, and/or co-workers who might be willing to write about you.
- Do not wait until the last minute to ask. Give references plenty of time and notice to write your letter of recommendation.
- Provide your references a deadline at least two weeks before your deadline. This deadline should be earlier than your official application deadline to give you a buffer.
- Provide those who will write your letter your updated *Scholar Profile* to help them write more accurately about you as a person. It will save them time or you have a tight deadline.
- Offer to provide them a draft a letter of recommendation and have them customize the letter. This might be an appealing proposition for busy professionals and one that

might help you to get your letter of recommendation back sooner.
- Thank everyone who wrote letters of recommendation for you.

Essays

Essays may be requested by some scholarship organizations as part of the scholarship application process. **Your essay might be the most important deciding factor on whether or not you are selected for a scholarship.** Commit early to writing engaging and compelling essays. The level of effort put into writing a winning essay will be worth it. Scholarship sponsors use the essay to learn more about you or your perspectives on topics important to the organization in ways academic performance (grades) and standardized test scores cannot reflect. Use your essay as an opportunity to showcase yourself and share information not conveyed previously on your application.

Thus, if a scholarship application requires an essay, write the essay! Do not fear writing essays. Follow the instructions carefully. The quickest way to get disqualified from selection is to deviate from following the instructions. If essay instructions specify a minimum or maximum word or character count, ensure you do not go over the maximum. If the scholarship entity provides a template or format, please use it. You should type the essay unless the instructions in the application indicate the essay should be handwritten.

Brainstorming

An effective way to begin writing an essay is to brainstorm. Brainstorming may seem tedious and unnecessary; however, it will save time and energy when composing your essay. Initially start by free writing and jotting down every thought you have without regard to organization, complete sentences, or immediate relevance. After a few iterations of brainstorming, read your brainstorming notes and highlight useful ideas and concepts that could be useful in your essay.

Sections of an Essay

Writing an essay can be difficult without an organized approach. Get organized by outlining the essay by breaking the essay into parts that can make it more manageable. Generally, there are three sections to an effective essay: introduction, body, and conclusion.

- **Introductory paragraph**: Includes a compelling hook and thesis statement that grabs the readers' attention and draws them in to keep reading. The hook should be bold and engaging to show your individuality and to ensure your essay stands out from the rest of the essays. The thesis statement contains three supporting points that act as a guide or roadmap that will be expanded on in the body of the essay. Make the thesis statement strong and ensure that you answer the essay question in a concise and focused manner.

- **Body paragraphs:** Develop a paragraph for each of the three supporting points specified in the thesis statement. The first paragraph should start with the strongest supporting point first. Include evidence that supports the thesis statement and expands on major themes. Also, share personal reflections and experiences in each of the supporting paragraphs.
- **Conclusion paragraph**: Restate the compelling hook and thesis statement. Then, summarize each supporting point in a separate sentence. Share any important information and conclude with the moral of the story and leave the reader with a lasting thought that relates to the theme of the essay and your personal experiences.

Essay Themes and Prompts

You may be instructed to write on a particular theme or topic or given the freedom to choose a specific theme or topic. In general, scholarship committees ask similar types of scholarship essay questions. Here are ten popular essay themes that can be used to answer a significant number of essay prompts or questions:

- Career or Professional
- Personal Statement
- Challenges
- Scholarship Need
- Change
- Character
- Leadership
- Community Service
- Contribution
- Creativity

Based on the scholarship essay themes, the scholar can develop essay prompts for various essay questions in advance of completing scholarship applications. Essay responses to the below questions could be drafted using the **Template 8: Scholarship Essay Prompt.** The essay prompts can be saved and reused for future scholarship essays.

Template 8: Scholarship Essay Prompt

ESSAY PROMPT

Essay Themes:

- ☐ Career or Professional
- ☐ Personal Statement
- ☐ Challenges
- ☐ Scholarship Need
- ☐ Change
- ☐ Character
- ☐ Leadership
- ☐ Community Service
- ☐ Contribution
- ☐ Creativity

Scholarship Essay Question:

_____

Thesis Statement: The main hook that addresses the theme or prompt. The thesis should make three supporting points. This sentence should be the first sentence in the introductory paragraph.

_____

Introductory Paragraph: Develop an engaging and compelling hook that describes the overall theme of the paper. Include the thesis statement in this paragraph.

_____

Body Paragraph 1: Draft one sentence for supporting point #1 identified in the thesis statement as the first sentence in each paragraph.

_____

Scholarship Essay Theme: *Career or Professional*

Share the scholar's career and future professional aspirations.

- What do you want to do after you graduate from college?
- Why did you select this career?
- How will you change the field/industry?
- Where do you see yourself five to ten years from now?
- Describe your most meaningful achievements and how they relate to your field of study and your future goals.

Scholarship Essay Theme: *Personal Statement*

Provide a summary of the scholar's life or an autobiography which typically describes information about the past, present, and future.

- Please write a short autobiography including information about your family, work experience, community involvement, hobbies, spare-time activities, and what you hope to do in the future.
- Please include a brief summary or personal statement describing your accomplishments and goals.
- List any honors and awards you have received.
- List your extra-curricular activities.

Scholarship Essay Theme: *Challenges*

Identify a time when the scholar experienced faced conflict, difficulty or hardship. Share how the scholar overcame challenges rather than give up, how the scholar rose to the occasion or what was learned to achieve success.

- Write a short essay that describes areas in your life where you demonstrated leadership and overcame obstacles either through your school, social, or family life.
- What's the most difficult challenge you've ever faced? How did you overcome it?

Scholarship Essay Theme: *Scholarship Need*

Describe why you need or want this scholarship. Consider financial, academic, and other needs.

- Why should you or earn the scholarship?
- Why do you need this scholarship?
- From a financial standpoint, what impact would this scholarship have on your education?
- State any special personal or family circumstances affecting your need for financial assistance.

Scholarship Essay Theme: *Change*

Provide insight on how the scholar would approach change. Share opinions, thoughts, and ideas on topics such as legislation, hunger, homelessness, education, the environment, etc. The Committees want to see analytical and critical thinking skills.

- What do you think we should do about gun control in this country?
- How would you handle texting and driving?
- Create an innovative solution to reduce waste.

Scholarship Essay Theme: *Character*

Share information on the scholar's character and what makes them who they are.

- Describe a time in your life that has shaped who you are as a person.
- How do you define success?
- What traits do you possess that will enhance your education or future career?
- Why are you a good candidate to receive this award?

Scholarship Essay Theme: *Leadership*

Share how the scholar exhibits leadership attributes in school, the community, and extracurricular activities.

- Describe how you have demonstrated leadership ability both in and out of school.
- Discuss a special leadership attribute or accomplishment that sets you apart.

Scholarship Essay Theme: *Community Service*

Describe the scholar's community service, community initiatives, and community improvement experience.

- Describe a meaningful volunteer or community service experience?

- Share a project you developed or implemented that impacted your school or community.

Scholarship Essay Theme: *Contribution*

Share the scholar's contribution to society or desire to make a difference.
- How will you make a difference in our world?
- How have you made a difference in your school and/or community?
- What do you think our country should do to foster unity?

Scholarship Essay Theme: *Creativity*

Share about the scholar's ability to be creative and innovative.
- Describe a situation or experience where you were creative and innovative.
- Create a video on a specific safety topic.

Useful Essay Writing Strategies:
- Start early and avoid last minute work.
- Use a positive and relatable tone.
- BE YOURSELF. Make sure your essay reflects who you are.

- Share inspirational personal experiences and examples to express how you were able to overcome hardships and difficulties.
- Address the essay topic or answer the question asked.
- Stick to the required word count minimum or maximum. Use your word processing software to confirm your word count.
- Brainstorm to generate ideas. Be creative.
- Do your research. Find out more about the scholarship entity, their vision/mission, and finding information specific to the scholarship topic. Researching will offer more content and perhaps make it easier to write the essay.
- Show your knowledge about the scholarship entity with relevant information, facts or statistics.
- Consider developing a brief outline to organize your thoughts.
- Develop your first draft and make sure your essay has three parts: (1) an introduction, (2) a body, and (3) a conclusion.
- Keep your topic narrow and focused. Don't cover too many topics.

- Avoid clichés. Don't rely on words or ideas others have previously used.
- Get feedback from someone who writes well (a parent or teacher). Have them edit your essay.
- Proofread and make corrections. Plan to write several drafts.

Test Scores

Some scholarship organizations require test scores (i.e. SAT/ACT). High test scores may qualify a scholar for collegiate or private merit-based scholarships. Scholars typically submit scores as part of the application process. Most scholars can select to send test scores to scholarship organizations when registering for the test or after the testing date. Based on provided instructions, send your official or unofficial test scores by logging onto the test organization's website and providing the scholarship organization-specific code to send your test scores. Some scholarship organizations may allow the scholar to self-report and provide official test scores later in the selection process.

Transcripts

When seeking college funding, some organizations may require the scholar to include a copy of their official or unofficial transcript. A transcript is a formal copy of a scholar's high school or college academic record including courses taken and the corresponding grades achieved, GPA per year and current cumulative GPA, as well as class demographics including the scholar's rank and class size.

Some scholarship sponsors may accept unofficial transcripts while others require official transcripts to be provided in a sealed envelope or sent directly from the high school or college to the requesting scholarship committee. Follow the exact instructions provided by the scholarship organization for transcript requests.

Moreover, you also need to understand your school's transcript request process and follow it precisely. Each school has its own process for transcript requests. Thus, it is critical to understand all the steps to obtain transcripts long before you need to request them. Some schools require permissions, waivers, and other forms to be complete. Some schools may offer a certain number of transcripts for free and other schools may charge a fee for each transcript. Find out ahead of time if there are transcript fees. If a scholar has an outstanding bill or fees with the school, the school may not release transcripts until the scholar's balance is paid in full. Parental permission may be required before a scholar can even request a high school transcript.

In some cases, it may take time to get these documents processed, so it will be crucial to know the process before you have to meet a short-term deadline. In fact, once you know the scholarship application requires a transcript, submit your request. This will ensure that your transcript will be sent on time or ahead of time. Based on experience, if transcripts and other documents are sent after the scholarship deadline, your application package may not be considered.

You can-check with the scholarship sponsor to ensure they have received your transcript before the deadline. If your transcript was not received, promptly follow-up with your school.

Track Your Progress

Develop a tracking checklist for all required documents and actions you must take for each application. Use a tracking tool to document submitted scholarship application information in one place such as this **Template 9: Funding/Scholarship Tracking Spreadsheet**. Also, keep a folder for all of your hard copy scholarship information.

Template 9: Funding/Scholarship Tracking Spreadsheet

Name: _____ Date: _____ EFC: _____ Need: _____

No	FUNDING/ SCHOLARSHIP NAME	APPLICATION LINK	ELIGIBILITY CRITERIA	AWARD AMOUNT	DEADLINE	ESSAY(S) (Y/N)	LETTER(S) OF RECOMMENDATION (Y/N)	TEST SCORES (Y/N)	DATE APPLICATION SUBMITTED	SELECTION DECISION	AMOUNT AWARDED	NOTES
1												
2												
3												
4												
5												

After applying for scholarships, you will likely receive correspondence from the scholarship sponsors to let you know if they selected you for the scholarship. You may receive notification by mail or email. If you receive scholarship funds, the sponsor may send the funds directly to you or directly to the college. If the funds are being sent directly to the college, be sure to provide the college you plan to attend the sponsor name, scholarship amount, and where possible when they should expect receipt. Be aware that your college might consider the additional scholarship funds as part of your financial aid package. If this happens, the college will adjust or reduce the amount of financial aid offered based on scholarship amounts received.

Successful Scholarship Application Strategies

1. **Begin early.** There is no reason to wait until your senior year to start applying for scholarships. The earlier you start, the more time you will have to research and fill out scholarship applications. Your goal is to submit the best possible scholarship application that you can.

2. **Apply for big and small scholarships.** Do not avoid applying for small scholarships. Some believe that small scholarships are not worth their time but smaller scholarships add up to help cover college costs.

3. **Write the scholarship essay, anyway.** Sometimes, scholars shy away from scholarship applications that require essays and that is a good reason for you to be the one to write the essay and apply. Take the time to develop a well-written essay. If your writing skills need improvement, consider working with someone who can help you strengthen your writing skills to develop a memorable essay.

4. **Differentiate yourself.** Leave a lasting impression on the scholarship selectors and differentiate yourself from other applicants. Let your personality and passion shine through your application and essay (if applicable). Highlight the special talents or skills you offer. Perhaps

share an experience you had that demonstrates your perseverance in the face of adversity as a scholar or leader. Also, consider sharing what makes you unique and/or your strengths. Find ways to stand out and leave an impression on those who may read your essay.

5. **Find a Scholarship Mentor.** Scholars compete for scholarships each year. Your goal is to align yourself with those who have been successful securing scholarships. I met a scholar who received over one million dollars in scholarships. When asked how she achieved that, she stated she went online, found past scholarship recipients and reached out to them to find out how they applied and how they wrote essays to differentiate themselves. Model yourself after others who have been successful at what you want to accomplish. Find the best models, study their strategies, and work to accomplish similar results.

6. **Pay attention to deadlines.** Be aware of scholarship and grant deadlines. Most scholarships and grants have a set deadline in which applicants can submit applications to receive funding for a particular academic school year. At the same time, some grants are only offered once a year and are awarded on a first-come, first-serve basis. If the application is not received by the deadline, the applicant

will likely have to wait until the next academic school year.

7. **Practice your interview skills.** Some scholarships require an in-person interview and interviewing requires practice. Take the necessary time to practice answering questions concisely about your background, interest, academic performance, leadership, unique talents, achievements, aspirations, and how you may have overcome adversity, as well as your plans for the future.

8. **Keep applying.** Keep searching and applying for scholarships while in high school and college. There are scholarships available for high school, vocational/trade, undergraduate, and graduate scholars. Chances are you will need funding each academic year until you complete your desired program. Therefore, develop a schedule to apply for scholarships until you graduate.

STRATEGY 9: MAXIMIZE YOUR TIME

"Yesterday is gone. Tomorrow has not yet come. We only have today. Let us begin." Mother Theresa

College funding planning involves different approaches, action steps, eligibility requirements, and deadlines. Timing is everything. To take advantage of the various college funding and financial aid approaches, it is important to understand what to do and when. It is imperative to incorporate timelines in your college funding plan, as well as keep track of the actions, requirements, and deadlines for each activity.

Since financial aid is awarded and distributed on a first come first serve basis, the earlier you apply, the more likely you are to understand your financial situation and get the financial aid you may need. To best determine what to do and when, follow the recommended college funding **Template 10: Timeline Checklists by Funding Stages** referenced in this book. The college funding timeline checklists are broken up by each of the four College Funding Stages (Early, Growth, Late, and Spending) and are further detailed by grade level in the Late Stage.

Template 10: Timeline Checklists by Funding Stages

Timeline Checklist (Early Stage)

- Start saving money for your child's education. Learn about tax advantages.
- Learn the basics of college costs and find out what college will cost.
- Find out how financial aid and scholarships can help cover college costs

Timeline Checklist (Growth Stage, K-7th Grade)

- Start saving money for your child's education, if you haven't already. Learn about tax advantages.
- Develop strong academic and study habits.
- Keep up your grades. Good grades not only expand your college opportunities but also can help you pay for college with scholarships and grants.
- Get involved in activities (playing sports, volunteering and participating in clubs). Activities can lead to scholarships that can make college more affordable.
- Learn the basics of college costs and find out what college will cost.

- Find out how financial aid and scholarships can help cover college costs. Keep in mind that you can apply for some scholarships starting in the Growth Stage.

<u>Middle School Scholars</u>:
- Develop a Scholar Profile. Start listing honors, awards, paid & volunteer work.
- Attend college and career fairs.
- Think about your college choices. Research and visit colleges (programs, requirements, costs). Check out this college search tool, College Navigator: <u>https://nces.ed.gov/collegenavigator/</u>.
- Think about your career options. Use a career search tool to complete a career interest assessment: <u>https://www.mynextmove.org/</u>.
- Begin your college planning journey. Check out the book <u>College Planning Strategies I Wish Someone Had Told Me</u> at: www.investnothers.com.

Timeline Checklist (Late Stage, 8th Grade)

- Learn the basics about the cost of college.
- Start saving money for college. Learn about tax efficient assets for college savings.
- Find out how financial aid and scholarships can help cover college costs. Keep in mind that you can apply for some scholarships now.
- Develop strong academic and study habits.
- Take challenging classes to prepare for high school.
- Talk with school counselors about high school college prep programs offered (i.e. AP courses, Governor schools, vocational schools, dual enrollment)
- Find out about high school programs and graduation requirements.
- Keep up your grades (3.0 GPA & above) and monitor your progress. Good grades not only expand your college opportunities but also can help you pay for college with scholarships and grants.
- Take an inventory of your interests and passions. Scholarships are not only based on academic achievement.

- Get involved in activities (playing sports, creative/performing arts, volunteering and participating in clubs). Activities can lead to scholarships that can make college more affordable.
- Research career options. Use a career search tool: https://www.mynextmove.org/.
- Attend college and career fairs.
- Begin your college planning journey. Check out the book <u>College Planning Strategies I Wish Someone Had Told Me</u> at: www.investnothers.com.

Timeline Checklist (Late Stage, 9th Grade)

Please note, many "Late Stage" checklist items will be repeated for each grade level. An asterisk indicates a new task to assist scholars in their preparation.

- Learn the basics about the cost of college.
- Start saving money for college, if you haven't already. Use tax and aid efficient assets for college savings.
- Discuss options and ideas to pay for college with your family.
- Develop your college funding plan. Most families use a combination of savings, current income and loans to pay their share of tuition and other costs.
- Budget for standardized tests, prep courses, college application fees, and other expenses needed before graduation.
- Begin your scholarship search plan.
- Develop and maintain strong academic and study habits.
- Find out about high school programs and graduation requirements.
- Consider taking courses with college credit or a college prep curriculum (AP courses, dual enrollment, and online courses).

- Keep up your grades (3.0 GPA & above) and monitor your progress. Good grades not only expand your college opportunities but also can help you pay for college with scholarships and grants.
- Prepare for standardized tests (i.e. SAT and ACT).
- Take an inventory of your interests and passions. Scholarships are not only based on academic achievement.
- Get involved in activities (playing sports, creative/performing arts, volunteering and participating in clubs). Activities can lead to scholarships that can make college more affordable.
- Develop a Scholar Profile. Start listing honors, awards, paid & volunteer work.
- List initial college options. Research and visit colleges (programs, requirements, costs). Check out this college search tool, College Navigator: https://nces.ed.gov/collegenavigator/.
- Research career options. Use a career search tool like: https://www.mynextmove.org/.
- Attend college and career fairs.

- Focus on the college admissions process. Check out the book College Planning Strategies I Wish Someone Had Told Me at: www.investnothers.com.

Timeline Checklist (Late Stage, 10th Grade)

Please note, many "Late Stage" checklist items will be repeated for each grade level. An asterisk indicates a new task to assist scholars in their preparation.

- Learn the basics about the cost of college. Attend Parent Financial Night or a College Funding and Financial Aid workshop.
- Start saving money for college, if you haven't already. Use tax and aid efficient assets for college savings.
- Discuss options and ideas to pay for college with your family.
- Develop or update your college funding plan. Most families use a combination of savings, current income and loans to pay their share of tuition and other costs.
- Budget for standardized tests, prep courses, college application fees, and other expenses needed before graduation.
- Continue your scholarship search plan.
- Identify individuals who can write letters of recommendation for scholarship applications.
- Develop and maintain strong academic and study habits.

- Find out about high school programs and graduation requirements.
- Consider taking courses with college credit or a college prep curriculum (AP courses, dual enrollment, and online courses).
- Keep up your grades (3.0 GPA & above) and monitor your progress. Good grades not only expand your college opportunities but also can help you pay for college with scholarships and grants.
- Prepare for standardized tests (i.e. SAT and ACT).
- Take the PSAT 10 (High school sophomore). Organizations such as the American Indian Graduate Center, Asian & Pacific Islander American Scholarship Fund, Hispanic Scholarship Fund, Jack Kent Cooke Foundation, and United Negro College Fund use the PSAT 10 to identify scholars for scholarships.
- Take an inventory of your interests and passions. Scholarships are not only based on academic achievement.
- Get involved in activities (playing sports, creative/performing arts, volunteering and participating

in clubs). Activities can lead to scholarships that can make college more affordable.

- Develop or update your Scholar Profile. Listing honors, awards, paid & volunteer work.
- Refine your list of initial college options. Research and visit colleges (programs, requirements, costs). Check out this college search tool, College Navigator: https://nces.ed.gov/collegenavigator/.
- Research career options. Use a career search tool like: https://www.mynextmove.org/.
- Attend college and career fairs.
- Focus on the college admissions process. Check out the book College Planning Strategies I Wish Someone Had Told Me at: www.investnothers.com.

Timeline Checklist (Late Stage, 11th Grade)

Please note, many "Late Stage" checklist items will be repeated for each grade level. An asterisk indicates a new task to assist scholars in their preparation.

- Learn the basics about the cost of college. Attend Parent Financial Night or a College Funding and Financial Aid workshop.
- Start saving money for college, if you haven't already. Use tax and aid efficient assets for college savings.
- Discuss options and ideas to pay for college with your family.
- Develop or update your college funding plan. Calculate a current estimate of your EFC using your base year taxes.
- Budget for standardized tests, prep courses, college application fees, and other expenses needed before graduation.
- Continue to implement your scholarship plan.
- Confirm your list of individuals you have identified to write letters of recommendation for scholarship applications. Be sure to provide them with your Scholar Profile, the recommendation letter template and any other information they require to write a recommendation when

requested.
- Verify you are on track to meet graduation requirements.
- Consider taking courses with college credit or a college prep curriculum (AP courses, dual enrollment, and online courses).
- Keep up your grades (3.0 GPA & above) and monitor your progress. Good grades not only expand your college opportunities but also can help you pay for college with scholarships and grants.
- Find out the transcript request process at your school. Request a copy of your official transcript.
- Take the PSAT/NMSQT (fall). High school juniors who take the PSAT/NMSQT are automatically entered into the National Merit Scholarship Program. Organization and colleges identify scholars based on their scores for admissions and scholarships.
- Schedule to take the SAT and ACT standardized tests (winter or spring). Take a prep in-person or online class to improve scores on standardized tests.
- Find out if the colleges on your list require standardized subject tests for admission.

- Take an inventory of your interests and passions. Scholarships are not only based on academic achievement.
- Get involved in activities (playing sports, creative/performing arts, volunteering and participating in clubs). Activities can lead to scholarships that can make college more affordable.
- Develop or update your Scholar Profile. Listing honors, awards, paid & volunteer work.
- Refine your list of initial college options. Research and visit colleges (programs, requirements, costs). Check out this college search tool, College Navigator: https://nces.ed.gov/collegenavigator/.
- Research career options. Use a career search tool like: https://www.mynextmove.org/.
- Attend college and career fairs.
- Focus on the college admissions process. Check out the book College Planning Strategies I Wish Someone Had Told Me at: www.investnothers.com.

Summer before 12th Grade:

- Register for your FSA ID (your parent will need a FSA ID also) from the Department of Education as you will need it to apply for the FAFSA at: FAFSA.gov
- Research outside scholarships and make a note of all deadlines on your Funding/Scholarship Tracking Spreadsheet. Pay close attention to DEADLINES!
  - Write scholarship essays (if applicable).
  - Request and obtain letters of recommendation.
- Register to take or <u>retake</u> the SAT or ACT college admissions standardized tests.
- Work and/or volunteer.
- Develop or update a Scholar Profile. List honors, awards, paid & volunteer work and other profile elements.
- Narrow down your career options and college options. Use a career search tools: CollegeBoard.org or https://www.mynextmove.org/.
- Review college applications and start drafting essays.
- Develop or update your college funding plan. Most families use a combination of savings, current income and loans to pay their share of tuition and other costs.

<u>Athletes</u>
- Complete your NCAA Certification Account (DIV I/DIV II)
- Send high school transcripts to NCAA Eligibility Center (after Junior year completed)

<u>Performers (Arts, Theater, Instrument, Vocal, Technical)</u>
- Determine audition/interview requirements
- Prepare a portfolio
- Add contests to Scholarship list.

Timeline Checklist (Late Stage, 12th Grade)

August – September (Start of Senior Year):

- Select your top colleges.
- Select your potential college major or field of study (or undecided).
- You (and your parents, if applicable) begin gathering financial documents (income, assets, and taxes).
- Register for your Federal Student Aid (FSA) ID (your parent will need an FSA ID also) from the Department of Education as you will need it to apply for the FAFSA at FAFSA.ed.gov.

September – December:

- Apply to your top colleges for early decision and early action deadlines. Pay close attention to DEADLINES!
- Write college essays (if applicable).
- Request and obtain letters of recommendation.
- Request your official transcripts (send to colleges).
- The Free Application for Federal Student Aid or <u>FAFSA</u> is available on October 1st. You can apply electronically at <u>FAFSA.ed.gov</u>.

- Complete the CSS/Financial Aid Profile for colleges that require it for early decision and early action at www.collegeboard.org.
- Complete any other institution specific aid applications
- Complete verification processes required by FAFSA, CSS Profile, or the college.
- Research and apply for outside scholarships and make a note of all deadlines on your Funding/Scholarship Tracking Spreadsheet. Pay close attention to DEADLINES!

- Write scholarship essays (if applicable).
- Request and obtain letters of recommendation.

Athletes only
- Update your NCAA Certification Account (DIV I/DIV II).
- Send official transcripts to NCAA the Eligibility Center (September of 12th-grade year).

Performers (Arts, Theater, Instrument, Vocal, Technical)
- Determine audition/interview requirements. Schedule auditions or interviews.
- Prepare a portfolio.
- Add contests to Scholarship list.

January – June:

- Continue applying for outside scholarships and make a note of all deadlines on your Funding/Scholarship Tracking Spreadsheet. Pay close attention to DEADLINES!
    - Write scholarship essays (if applicable).
    - Request and obtain letters of recommendation.
- Compare your financial aid awards. The colleges you apply to will send financial aid award letters by April which will reflect how much and which kinds of aid they are offering you. Your college funding planning specialist can help you make side-by-side comparisons of each college's aid package or you can use the Compare Your Aid Awards calculator at: https://bigfuture.collegeboard.org/pay-for-college/financial-aid-awards/compare-aid-calculator.
- Notify your selected college as soon as you solidify your decision, and no later than know the college's deadline. The deadline for most colleges is May 1st.
- Select the elements of your financial aid award you choose to accept by the deadline. Financial aid is limited and is awarded on a first come first serve

basis. If you miss the deadline, your gift aid award may go to another scholar. You can, however, ask for an extension if you are waiting to hear from other schools. Each college will decide if it will give you an extension.
- Pay applicable college deposits and fees by the deadline for housing, meals, and other fees.
- Graduate and Celebrate!
- Register for college courses, if the college permits early registration.
- Send the final high school transcript to your selected college.
- June 30th – If you have not filed the FAFSA for the upcoming academic year, you may only qualify for federal aid.

Athletes only
- Update your NCAA Certification Account (DIV I/DIV II).
- Send final transcripts to the NCAA Eligibility Center (End of 12th-grade year)
- **July/August (Start of College):**

- Develop a checklist of items needed for college and purchase them over the summer. If you wait until the scholar goes to college, this could be quite expensive.
- Prepare to pay the college tuition bill or make payment arrangements, if your costs are not otherwise paid. Costs are billed by the semester.

Timeline Checklist (Spending Stage)

- Note: If you are planning to apply for vocation/college admission, follow the LATE Stage (12th Grade) checklist for more detailed guidance.
- Work and save money for college, if you haven't already. Saving some money will help with expenses. Learn about tax advantages.
- You (and your parents, if applicable) begin gathering financial documents (income, assets, and taxes).
- Register for your FSA ID (your parent will need an FSA ID also) from the Department of Education as you will need it to apply for the FAFSA at FAFSA.gov.
- The Free Application for Federal Student Aid or FAFSA is available on October 1st. The last day to file the FAFSA for the upcoming academic year is June 30th.
- Submit your FAFSA by the financial aid deadline for existing students usually no later than March 1st.
- Accept your desired financial aid award elements by the deadline. Financial aid is limited and is awarded on a first come first serve basis, or your award may go to another scholar.

- Complete financial aid paperwork. If loans are part of your financial aid package, you'll have to complete and submit paperwork to get the money.
- Pay applicable college deposits and fees by the deadline for housing, meals, and other fees.
- Register for college courses, if early registration is permitted.
- Prepare to pay the college tuition bill or make payment arrangements if your costs are not otherwise paid. Costs are billed by semester.
- Keep your grades up (3.0 GPA & above) and monitor your progress. Scholarships continue to be available and you may have to meet minimum GPA requirements to keep awarded scholarships and for new scholarships.
- Develop or update a Scholar Profile or resume.
- Continue researching and applying for outside scholarships and make a note of all deadlines on your Funding/Scholarship Tracking Spreadsheet. Pay close attention to due dates and deadlines!
  - Write scholarship essays (if applicable).
  - Request and obtain letters of recommendation.
  - Find out the transcript request process at your school.

STRATEGY 10: EXECUTE YOUR FUNDING PLAN

"Always plan ahead. It wasn't raining when Noah built the ark."
Richard Cushing

Regardless of the college funding stage you are in, one of the most important actions you could take is developing and executing a college funding plan. The earlier you start the better positioned you will be to pay less out of your pocket for college. Unless you have the total cost of your college expenses covered or fully paid for, make developing a college funding plan your priority. Establishing an effective college funding plan is critical. If you are seeking financial assistance or support from parents, guardians, and/or other supporters, include them in the planning process. The process of creating your plan will reveal where there are gaps to fill to aid in your success.

Middle and high school scholars and their parents should not wait until their junior or senior year of high school to begin. Scholars currently in college or those considering getting advanced degrees should start executing a funding plan also. The point is, any scholar who intends to pursue higher education must take advantage of the time they have to develop and execute an effective plan. Waiting until you know the exact college you will attend, your exact major or career field or the exact cost of college attendance will not serve your interest to reduce the amount of out-of-pocket expenses and possibly graduate debt-free. Start early and finish strong. Get educated, get organized, and get to work!

College Funding Plan

You are now equipped to develop your college funding plan. Your **Template 11: College Funding Plan** should be customized based on your specific needs and funding situation. Plan on updating your college funding plan annually.

Template 11: College Funding Plan

Name:_____ Enrollment Date:_____ College Funding Stage:_____

EFC:_____ Need:_____ College Funding Approach:_____

No.	Activity	Type	Cost	Start Date	End Date	% Complete	Results	Notes
1								
2								
3								
4								
5								

The template for your plan is meant to be simple, so as not to overwhelm you. As a caution, do not over complicate your plan because it may be difficult to implement. Your funding plan should include information on key activities or actions you need to take, costs and expenses for each activity, start and due dates, percent completion, results accomplished, and any items or important details to note.

- Leverage this college funding plan and build it out based on how you plan to implement the previous strategies outlined in this book.

Get Organized

As you develop a college funding plan, get organized. At the same time, getting organized will be important throughout the college funding process. Organization skills are essential to stay on track and accomplish your goals on time. Scholars should develop a system or approach that works for them to (1) manage electronic files and hard copy information, paperwork, and documents as well as (2) manage website and application usernames and passwords.

The best way to do this is to spend a few minutes developing a system or approach that works best for the scholar.

Electronic and/or Paper Copy Filing System:

Another aspect of planning is figuring out where to put your documents so that you can retrieve them with ease later. Establish an electronic and paper filing system for current and future materials with a naming convention (with the date you stored them) to help you intuitively find documents information easily. Store and save documents in the same places consistently. Consider setting up folders for each key document type as well as saving electronic versions of your documents with a date. This will help you to find documents and access the latest version with ease.

Getting organized and developing an effective college funding plan can make a significant difference. By establishing a plan, navigating the funding process will be manageable. Additionally, you can manage your time and resources (including money) more effectively and track progress easily. Decide early how you will categorize information and documentation and then establish a paper and electronic filing system. Some files or folders might include:

- College Funding Plan
- Financial Aid
- Income and Tax Documents

- Scholarships
- Current School Information
- Transcripts
- Test Scores
- Letters of Recommendation
- Essays
- Activities
- Scholar Profile/Resume
- Colleges

Username and Password Management:

Managing username and password information may seem self-intuitive, but it still needs addressing. As a scholar navigates through the college funding process, there will be numerous online websites and portals that will require a unique login username and password information.

Managing username and passwords for numerous sites can be a challenge. Therefore, it is recommended to keep a log of your login information in a safe place that is accessible for the scholar and parents/guardians who may be assisting in the process. The goal is to store your login information in a manner that you can retrieve it easily. There is nothing like needing to gain access to a system quickly but not being able to find the correct login information. If a parent is working with a scholar, make sure the parent and the scholar have access to the username and password information. Consider establishing a joint email address to ensure you view and respond to important information promptly.

Consider Your College Funding Stage

Your college funding plan should align with the actions you should take for your college funding stage. If you are in the Early Stage, you have more time to plan than someone in the Late or Spending Stage. Allow more or less time to accomplish tasks in each stage. It is always better to plan early and start when your scholar is in elementary or middle school using estimates as if your current financial and household situation was the same as when your scholar will be a senior in high school.

Adjust your plan when your scholar enters high school, at the second semester sophomore year (the beginning of the "base year" for income reporting), and finally, during the summer before senior year. By October of their senior year in high school, you should be well prepared to secure need-based aid and/or pay the out-of-pocket cost of the affordable colleges where your scholar gets accepted. Additionally, the scholar should have pursued, be pursuing, and continue to pursue scholarship resources.

If you are in the Late Stage, you now have what you need to plan from where you are. Focus, persistence, and consistency are what you need to maximize the opportunity for receiving "other people's money." You should also be efficient in how you spend your resources. No matter if you are in high school, college, or a graduate program, always be looking for scholarships/free money - at least until you have no more personal out-of-pocket costs or do not have to rely on even student loans.

CONCLUSION

"I think a college education is important no matter what you do in life." Phil Mickelson

Finding and getting accepted into affordable colleges is half the battle. One of the most challenging aspects of getting accepted and attending college is determining how to pay for it. Finding college funding may be one of the most important factors affecting whether or not a scholar will graduate or complete his or her program. Out-of-pocket payments, financial aid, grants, and scholarships are typical ways to fund college.

Without enough funding, some scholars and parents stress and struggle with how to cover the cost of attendance. Some scholars continue to pursue their educational dreams by graduating deeply in debt. Whether the scholar is pursuing higher education to attend a vocational or trade school, two-year college, four-year college, or graduate school, learning to navigate the college funding process will help scholars make their college graduation dreams come true!

Since everyone's financial situation is different, use the college funding strategies and templates outlined in this book to achieve your goals. The college funding strategies will help scholars understand how to develop and implement an effective college funding plan, based on his or her specific College Funding Stage, to reduce or eliminate cost of out-of-pocket expenses.

Use the templates provided in this book to assist in your college funding endeavors. Download the templates from our websites and customize them as you desire. Also, in the Appendices of this book, there are additional college funding websites and books that you might find helpful.

The earlier a scholar decides to pursue higher education, the more likely they are to successfully fund college without going broke. The sooner you begin to plan, ideally in the Early Stage, the more time you will have to deliberately and strategically fund college. If you are in the Late or Spending Stage, do not get discouraged. There is still time. Stay encouraged, work your specific plan, and do not give up on the process. You can also graduate debt-free!

College funding and planning professionals can assist with (but not limited to) (1) college planning, (2) scholarship searches and applications, (3) financial planning and savings, (4) financial aid, (5) essay writing, and more. Sure, you may have to make an initial investment by paying for the professional services you need; however, the return on your investment could pay dividends. For example, if you solicit professional services that initially cost you $400 and through the help of professionals you can fund college at $20,000 or more a year for four years, then it would be worth the initial investment of $400. Receiving college funding assistance may help you to find funding to cover four years of college at $80,000 or more.

If you need college funding support from a college funding planning professional, please contact the following individuals for assistance:

Christie Chamblis Murray, DBA
College Planning and Scholarship Expert: Contact Dr. Murray for assistance with college admissions counseling and planning. Dr. Murray also assists scholars with developing their scholarship search and application plan. Dr. Murray provides educational workshops on the College Planning Process and Scholarship Planning for organizations that serve scholars and their parents.
Email: Author.christiemurray@investnothers.com

Nicole Cole, MBA

<u>Certified College Funding Planning Specialist:</u> Contact Ms. Cole for assistance with developing and implementing your college funding plan including estimated EFC calculation, COA and need comparisons, choosing your approach, special funding circumstances, aid application support, aid award comparisons, and plans to pay your out-of-pocket costs. Ms. Cole also provides educational workshops on "College Funding and Financial Aid" for organizations that serve scholars and parents.

<u>Email</u>: Nicole@collegemoneylady.com

Do not just "go" to college. **Go and Graduate Debt-free**! This will require focus, self-discipline, and effective study skills to achieve the academic success scholars seek. Chances are, you will discover things you never knew about yourself. Also, when you have an opportunity to help, reach back and assist others to move forward too! Share this book and other useful resources with others who wish someone had told them!

~THANK YOU AND BEST WISHES~

TESTIMONIALS

Joli Cooper-Nelson
5th National President
Jack and Jill of America, Inc.

As a parent of three, a working mother, and community leader, being able to fund my children's college education was imperative. Nicole Cole, with The College Money Team, helped us understand the college funding process, financial aid, and how to leverage our resources to support eight years of college costs. More importantly, over the last four years, Nicole has effectively navigated and guided us specific to our special circumstances including transitioning between careers, transferring colleges, and aid related to a college athlete.

Having a background in the financial industry, believe me when I say, college funding is different. What's also different is a scholar (and parent) getting through senior year in high school. Preparing for, applying to and funding college, was one of the most stressful, laborious, and expensive times for our family. I highly recommend hiring a professional like Nicole to get through it. Nicole lightened our load significantly. We now have one scholar about to graduate and another a year away from graduating from an

Ivy League college. Moreover, and largely due to college funding planning with Nicole, we did not devastate our household finances to get it done.

U. S. Navy, Ensign Sherman Grant
Hampton University 2019 Graduate

College planning is an essential key to one's college future. To get where one desires to be in life, some sort of planning has to be in that process. With the help of my cousin, Dr. Christie Chamblis Murray, I was grateful to have her support with choosing where to go to college and finding money to pay for college. She was an alumna of my number one college choice, Hampton University.

The cost to attend Hampton University, at that time was and still is, very expensive. Dr. Murray shared college planning and funding strategies with me and my parents throughout my senior year of high school. During this time, she stated that I needed to find a way to pay for college and that I should apply for different scholarships to offset the cost of attendance and graduate debt-free.

She offered proven college strategies on how to apply to colleges and find scholarships. I was interested in the Navy ROTC and Army ROTC scholarships, which covered full-tuition, books, room and board, and being commissioned as an officer after graduation. I was also interested in the Hampton University National Alumni Scholarship that covered additional costs. Dr. Murray stressed that I should apply for numerous scholarships and that I could only get a "yes" or "no" response when applying for scholarships! She shared that I needed to put all my effort and energy into each scholarship application.

I received over $130,000 in scholarship funding and benefits. I was able to choose between the Navy and Army ROTC scholarships. I chose the Navy ROTC scholarship which offered four years of college tuition, books, and room and board. It also included employment and an officer commission in the U.S. Navy upon my college graduation. I had no out-of-pocket expenses for my college education and I graduated without student loans.

Thanks to Dr. Murray's support, guidance, and expertise, I graduated from Hampton University, May 12, 2019 debt-free. Her college planning and funding support helped me accomplish all of my academic goals. I was able to go to the college of my choice, graduate debt-free from a prestigious private university, and obtain my commission as an Ensign in the United States Navy. If you follow Dr. Murray's proven strategies, so can you!

Edward L. Tarlton, PhD
Executive Director & Founder
HELP Consulting, LLC 501c (3)

My non-profit, HELP Consulting, LLC, works with scholars from around the country to achieve their higher education goals whether a Bachelor's, Master's, or Doctorate is in their sights. While we support our clients in all areas of the admissions process and to be successful while they are pursuing their degree, we have relied on The College Money Team and Nicole Cole, MBA, specifically, for her expertise in financial aid and college funding planning. We have trusted Ms. Cole since 2009 to work with our client families, one-on-one, to help them understand the college funding process, financial aid qualification and resources.

Different from a university financial aid officer, Ms. Cole has worked with our clients to create a strategy to receive aid where possible, plan for efficient use of their financial resources and support the scholars to create their scholarship search and application plan. Mostly for HELP, Ms. Cole has been an educator for our clients. From 2016 to 2018, we engaged Ms. Cole to present online College Funding and Financial Aid live webinars to our Apply Texas Bootcamp - Youth Adventure Program (YAP) students and their parents.

Where HELP Consulting has aided scholars in being successful with admissions through persistence to graduation, Ms. Cole aids the scholar and family in being financially successful towards their degree goal.

APPENDIX A: WEBSITE RESOURCES

In this Appendix you can find other website resources on college funding, financial aid, and scholarships. These website resources will help you to use your time wisely by not having to start from scratch to find valuable information. The website links provided in this book may change, break, or get redirected by the website content owners. If the links provided do not work, please use an Internet and perform searches to find the correct link.

General College Funding Information

- Invest N Others LLC: https://www.investnothers.com/college-planning
- The College Money Team: http://thecollegemoneyteam.com/

Financial Aid

- An Ultimate Guide to Understanding Financial Aid: https://www.usnews.com/education/best-colleges/paying-for-college/articles/an-ultimate-guide-to-understanding-college-financial-aid?int=undefined-rec

- College Board Institutional Aid Application: https://cssprofile.collegeboard.org/
- Department of Education - Free Application for Financial Student Aid: https://fafsa.ed.gov
- Sallie Mae: https://www.salliemae.com/research/how-america-pays-for-college/

EFC Calculators
- Student Aid: https://studentaid.gov/understand-aid/estimate
- College Board: https://bigfuture.collegeboard.org/pay-for-college/paying-your-share/expected-family-contribution-calculator#efc_status

Award Letter Comparison Calculators
- College Covered: https://www.collegecovered.com/award-letter-tool/
- Discover: https://www.discover.com/student-loans/calculators/award-letter-comparison-tool
- Fast Web College Gold: http://www.collegegold.com/applydecide/lettercomparison

- Fin Aid: https://www.finaid.org/calculators/awardletter.phtml

Scholarships
- Air Force ROTC: https://www.afrotc.com/scholarships
- Army ROTC: https://www.goarmy.com/rotc/scholarships.html
- Cappex: https://www.cappex.com/
- College Board: www.bigfuture.collegeboard.org
- College Scholarships: www.collegescholarships.com/
- CollegeXpress: https://www.collegexpress.com/scholarships/search
- Fastweb: www.fastweb.com
- Naval ROTC: http://www.nrotc.navy.mil/scholarships.html
- Niche: https://www.niche.com/colleges/scholarships/?niche=niche-scholarships
- Peterson's: https://www.petersons.com/scholarship-search.aspx
- Scholarships.com: https://www.scholarships.com/

- Scholarship Search Best Practices: https://www.collegexpress.com/articles-and-advice/financial-aid/articles/scholarships-grants-loans/scholarship-search-best-practices/
- Scholly: www.myscholly.com
- Student Aid Scholarships: https://studentaid.ed.gov/sa/types/grants-scholarships/finding-scholarships
- Student Scholarships.org: https://studentscholarships.org/#sthash.BzlEVpBW.dpbs
- The 10 Best Scholarship Books: https://www.bestcollegereviews.org/best-scholarship-books/
- The Scholarship System: http://thescholarshipsystem.com/home
- Ultimate Guide: How to Find and Secure Scholarships for College: https://www.usnews.com/education/best-colleges/paying-for-college/articles/how-to-find-and-secure-scholarships-for-college
- Scholarship.com: www.Scholarships.com

- U.S. Department of Labor:
  www.careerinfonet.org/scholarshipsearch

Career and College Search Tools

- College Navigator:
  https://nces.ed.gov/collegenavigator/
- My Next Move: https://www.mynextmove.org/

College Planning

- Cappex College Search: https://www.cappex.com/
- College and Career Ready:
  https://www.collegeandcareerready.org
- College Data: https://www.collegedata.com/
- College Ranking: https://www.usnews.com/education
- Education Planner: http://www.educationplanner.org/
- I'm First Plan: http://www.imfirst.org/2012/12/plan/
- Invest N Others LLC: www.investnothers.com
- Kaplan Factors in College Admission:
  https://www.kaptest.com/college-prep/applying-to-college/key-factors-in-college-admissions
- Opportunities: Preparing for College:
  https://ecmc.org/opportunities

- Peterson's Timeline: https://www.petersons.com/college-search/planning-list-students-parents.aspx
  - studypoint.com

Essay Writing
- 10 Tips to Inspire College Essays: https://www.usnews.com/education/best-colleges/slideshows/10-tips-to-inspire-college-essays
- Big Future, Best College Essay: https://bigfuture.collegeboard.org/get-in/essays/8-tips-for-crafting-your-best-college-essay
- College Express, College Essay: https://www.collegexpress.com/articles-and-advice/admission/articles/college-applications/writing-college-application-essay/
- Common Essay Topics: https://www.usnews.com/education/best-colleges/articles/2018-07-09/what-admissions-officers-think-of-3-common-college-essay-topics?int=undefined-rec

- Eight Steps Towards a Better Scholarship Essay: https://www.internationalstudent.com/essay_writing/scholarship_essay/
- How to Write a Scholarship Essay Introduction (With Example): https://scholarshipowl.com/blog/apply-for-scholarships/scholarship-essay-introduction/
- How to Write a Thesis Statement for a Scholarship Essay: https://blog.csb.uncw.edu/how-to-write-a-thesis-statement-for-a-scholarship-essayPrinceton College Essay Advice: https://www.princetonreview.com/college-advice/college-essay
- Top 5 Items to List in Your Scholarship Essay: http://scholarshipmentor.com/top-5-items-list-your-scholarship-essay
- The 16 Most Popular Scholarship Essay and Application Questions: https://scholarshipinformer.com/popular-scholarship-essay-and-application-questions/
- USA News, How to Write a College Essay: https://www.usnews.com/education/best-colleges/articles/how-to-write-a-college-essay

- Useful Tricks on How to Write a Scholarship Essay: https://college-homework-help.org/blog/how-to-write-a-scholarship-essay

NCAA Eligibility for Scholar-athletes

- National Collegiate Athletic Association: http://www.ncaa.org/about/student-athlete-eligibility
- NCAA Eligibility Center: http://www.ncaa.org/student-athletes/future/eligibility-center
- NCAA Recruiting Calendar: http://www.ncaa.org/student-athletes/resources/recruiting-calendars/2017-18-division-i-and-ii-recruiting-calendars

SAT and ACT Testing

- ACT: https://www.act.org
- College Board (SAT): https://www.collegeboard.org
- College Board (SAT): https://www.collegeboard.org
- Free Test Prep: http://www.freetestprep.com
- Huntington Test Prep: https://huntingtonhelps.com/test-prep

- Kaplan: https://www.kaptest.com
- Khan Academy: https://www.khanacademy.org
- Kent Prep: https://kentprep.com
- Princeton Review: https://www.princetonreview.com
- Review.com: http://www.reviews.com/act-sat-test-prep-courses/
- Power Score: https://www.powerscore.com/act/courses/
- PrepScholar: https://prepscholar.com/sat/s/
- Spark Notes: http://www.sparknotes.com/testprep/
- Study Point: https://www.

APPENDIX B: BOOK RESOURCES

- <u>1001 Ways to Pay for College</u> (Gen & Kelly Tanabe)
- <u>50 Successful Harvard Application Essays: What Worked for Them Can Help You Get into the College of Your Choice</u> (Harvard)
- <u>College Planning Strategies I Wish Someone Had Told Me</u> (Dr. Christie Chamblis Murray)
- <u>Confessions of a Scholarship Winner: The Secrets that Helped Me Win $500,000 in Free Money for College – How You Can Too!</u> (Kristina Ellis)
- <u>Countdown to College: 21 'To Do' Lists for High School</u> (Valerie Pierce & Cheryl Rilly)
- <u>Debt-Free U: How I Paid for an Outstanding College Education Without Student Loans, Scholarships or Mooching Off My Parents</u> (Zac Bissonnette)
- <u>Fiske Guide to Colleges 2019</u> (Edward Fiske)
- <u>Get Free Cash for College</u> (Gen Tanabe and Kelly Tanabe)
- <u>Go to College for Free: College Planning ABC's Guide to Finding Scholarships, Financial Aid and Free Tuition Awards for College</u> (Manuel & Sterling Fabriquer Publishing Group)

- Homeschooling High School: Planning Ahead for College Admission (New and Updated) (Dennis and Jeanne Gowen)
- How to Be a High School Superstar: A Revolutionary Plan to Get into College by Standing Out (Without Burning Out) (Newport, Cal)
- How to Get Your Child into College: The Parents' Guide to College Planning (Felice Douglas)
- How to Go to College Almost for Free (Ben Kaplan)
- How to Send Your Student to College Without Losing Your Mind or Your Money (Howard, Shellee)
- How to Write a Winning Scholarship Essay: 30 Essays That Won Over $3 Million in Scholarships (Gen & Kelly Tanabe)
- Paying for College Without Going Broke, 2017 Edition: How to Pay Less for College (College Admissions Guides) (Princeton Review & Kalman Chany)
- Peterson's Scholarships, Grants, & Prizes (Peterson)
- Scholarships 101: The Real-World Guide to Getting Cash for College (Kimberly Ann Stezala)
- Scholarship Handbook (The College Board)

- <u>The Financial Aid Handbook: Getting the Education You Want for the Price You Can Afford</u> (Carol Stack and Ruth Vedvik)
- <u>The Scholarship & Financial Aid Solution: How to Go to College for Next to Nothing with Short Cuts, Tricks and Tips from Start to Finish</u> (Debra Lipphardt)
- <u>The Ultimate Scholarship Book: Billions of Dollars in Scholarships, Grants, and Prizes</u> (Gen Tanabe and Kelly Tanabe)
- <u>The Ultimate College Preparation Blueprint: Everything You Should Expect and Do When Planning for College</u> (Christopher Lewis)
- <u>What High Schools Don't Tell You</u> (Elizabeth Wissner)
- <u>Winning Scholarships for College</u> (Marianne Ragins)
- <u>Write Your Way to a Successful Scholarship Essay</u> (Candace Chambers)

CPSIA information can be obtained
at www.ICGtesting.com
Printed in the USA
FSHW020049140420
69127FS